Published in 2012

Praxis Studios

Praxis Studios
5205 Prospect Rd. 135-145
San Jose, CA 95129

Distributed by Needlework Arts
A subsidiary of Praxis Studios
www.needleworkarts.com

Printed in China

2012

Library of Congress Control Number 2011908677

ISBN 978-0-615-47875-3

10 9 8 7 6 5 4 3 2

# Holiday Boutique Knitting

Inspired Holiday Décor and Gifts to Knit

Mary Jean Daigneault

This book is dedicated to my Mom for teaching me everything, including how to knit and to my Dad, for making sure that I understood that I could accomplish anything I set my mind to.

I want to thank my friends, Libbie and Minnie who graciously allowed me to photograph some of my items in their beautiful homes. I'm grateful for their love and unwavering faith in me always. I want to thank my friend, Maureen who doesn't think she did anything, but who God chose to work through, by bringing to me, the people needed to make this book.

I put a lot of trust in my graphic artist, Elise McDougall, who has lived up to all expectations. She is incredibly creative, knowledgeable and terrific to work with. I look forward to working with her in the future. I am so grateful for my daughter Alana and her two friends, Kate and Kimberly, who were amazingly intuitive models and made shooting their pictures, the easiest part of the book!

I would like to express my gratitude to my sister LuAnn, for helping to edit this book and supporting me through everything I do.

I want to give a shout out to my crafting friends. Every year we take a weekend and get away to a house on a lake, hauling our crafting/knitting supplies with us. It is our reprieve from the holiday hassles and has become less about crafting and more about enjoying time with good friends. Thank you for your support and encouragement. I love you all.

My thanks are never ending for the love and support that I received from my husband Kevin and my daughter, Alana. I could not have pulled this book off without them stepping up to the plate and picking up the slack. Thanks for eating quick meals and leftovers. Thanks for putting up with Christmas decor intruding into our space and my constant knitting through everything. My daughter, Alana, is my greatest joy, and I am eternally grateful for her presence in my life, on a daily basis. She is the most creative soul I know and is the wind beneath my wings.

# Contents

# ··· Introduction

Inspiration to create this book came from my love of knitting, my love of Christmas, and my love of decorating with beautiful holiday décor that can transform our homes into a fantastical, festive world. Holiday Boutique Knitting is a compilation of holiday décor and gift patterns, designed to be fun to make, for you and for others.

The projects contained in this book are created with an artistic eye, and a vision of how they will occupy interior spaces. Fabricated to take on life, as unexpected, tasteful knitted décor, these pieces have been designed to stand the test of time, while also holding their own amongst their contemporary peers. They are transitional in design, and will fit into any interior style.

Designer tips throughout the book offer useful advice to successfully incorporate any of these projects into your holiday interiors. Interior designer secrets are included to stimulate creative ideas necessary to decorate for the holidays with confidence. The decorating tips help to grow your knitting practice, armed with solid advice to confidently choose yarns, based on colors and textures that make your projects unique and even more fun to knit.

Patterns in this book range from easy, impressive projects that are enjoyable for beginners, as well as seasoned knitters, to intermediate projects with easy to follow instructions with which beginners can grow.

Unique, handmade gifts are the most heartfelt presents that we can offer our friends and family. Some of this artful knitted décor would be a welcomed donation for your favorite fundraiser. I truly hope that these patterns bring you much pleasure.

It is the continuum, the traditions that connect us for generations. Hopefully this book will inspire you to design your dream holiday environment and create some of the projects highlighted throughout the pages for yourself and others. I wish you joyous holidays, year after year, for you and your loved ones.

# ··· Christmas Décor

To de-stress and un-complicate our holidays is a good thing. It is desirable to keep holiday time sacred, for praying, reflecting and enjoying our families and friends. Occurring only once a year, this special time goes by quickly, which becomes ever more apparent as we watch our children grow at stupendous speed. The few years that is our childhood, becomes our barometer with which to judge all future Christmases. Childhood experiences largely influence the traditions we enact as heads of our own family.

Decorations carry sentimental value. Tradition and memories are forever linked with certain treasured pieces. Every year we are given an opportunity to assess our décor collection and weed out what we no longer want or what we have outgrown. Evaluation of our stash is in order. Décor for the current year will be pulled out and pieces that do not fit with this years plan will be lovingly stored for future use. Planning may also dictate, what, if any new décor is necessary to purchase for the present year.

# Mr. and Mrs. Snow

• • •

*The man in the tuxedo holds the large microphone up to his face and begins the introduction, "Ladies and Gentlemen it is my greatest honor to introduce to you the well-dressed stars of tonight's show, the illustrious Mr. and Mrs. Snow!!!" The crowd goes wild, as the bright light follows the fluffy and, well, let's be honest, bulbous duo as they slide ever so gracefully to the middle of the stage.*

*Put this two foot high couple, in a well-deserved vignette and you will be guaranteed to get attention and applause from old and young alike. These celebrities are irresistible to folks of all ages. It is common to see people congregate around these superstars, as the paparazzi shoot away, lights flashing.*

• • •

This project is not only extremely impactful, rating very high on the humdinger chart, it is also very easy and quick to make. Don't let the length of the directions scare you off. They are written to be concise and easy to follow. Feel free to customize this project by using yarns that are appropriate for your color scheme. This snow couple is an adorable addition to any Christmas décor and will be remembered by the children as a favorite decoration for years to come. Enjoy making Mr. and Mrs. Snow come to life.

# Mr. and Mrs. Snow

NOTE: Increases are made by knitting into the front and back of the stitch.

## MATERIALS

- Yarn:

  1 Skein, 100% Natural Alpaca Weight

  3 ply 5oz. 604 yds

  2 Skeins, White Worsted Weight Yarn

  4 Skeins, White Fun Fur Skeins

  1 Skein, Lamb's Pride Worsted

  85%Wool/15%Mohair

  4oz. (113 Grams) 190 years

- Circular Needles Size US #11 / 8.0mm

  5 dpn's #11/ 8.0mm

  US #7 / 4.5mm

## MATERIALS FOR SNOW PERSON STRUCTURE

- 30mm Animal Eyes

- 2 branches for arms

- Cotton yarn to wrap around branch

- 3 Styrofoam balls: 1 - 10" ball 25.4cm;
  Two 8" balls 20.3 cm

- 5/16" x 36" Dowel – Make sure it fits
  into the bushing

- ¾" x 3/8" Galvanized Hex Bushing

- 3/8" x 1/8" Galvanized Hex Bushing

- ¾" NPT flange 3-1/2" diameter

- Hot glue gun

- Measuring tape or ruler

- Box Cutter

- 3" & 4" diameter bowl or glass to trace onto balls

- Serrated large bread knife

- Candle

  Gauge: 4" = 13 rows; 4" = 13 sts.

## MAKING MR. AND MRS. SNOW

**Using yarn A and yarn B held together:**

**Cast on 30 sts loosely**

Row 1 and every odd row:  K to end

Row 2: *K4, inc1; rep from * to end (36 sts)

Row 4: *K5, inc1; rep from * to end (42 sts)

Row 6: *K6, inc1; rep from * to end (48 sts)

Row 8: *K7, inc1; rep from * to end (54 sts)

Row 10: *K8, inc1; rep from * to end (60 sts)

Row 12: *K9, inc1; rep from * to end (66 sts)

Row 14: *K10, inc1; rep from * to end (72 sts)

Row 16: *K 11, inc1; rep from * to end (78 sts)

Row 18: *K12, inc1; rep from * to end (84 sts)

Row 20: *K13, inc1; rep from * to end (90 sts)

Rows 22: *K14, inc1; rep from * to end (96 sts)

Rows 24 –28 and every even row: *K to end

Row 29: *K10, k2tog; rep from * to end (88 sts)

Row 31: *K9, k2tog; rep from * to end (80 sts)

Row 33: *K8, k2tog; rep from * to end (72 sts)

Row 35: *K7, k2tog; rep from * to end (64 sts)

Row 37: *K6, k2tog; rep from * to end (56 sts)

Row 39: *K5, k2tog; rep from * to end k4 (48 sts)

Row 41: *K2, k2tog; rep from * to end (36 sts)

Rows 43 – 48: K to end

Row 49:  *K2, inc 1; rep from * to end (48 sts)

Row 51: *K11, inc 1; rep from * to end (52 sts)

Row 53: *K12, inc 1; rep from * to end (56 sts)

Row 55: *K13, inc 1; rep from * to end (60 sts)

Row 57: *K14, inc 1; rep from * to end, (64 sts)

Row 58 – 65: K to end

Row 66: *K14, k2tog; rep from * to end, (60sts)

Row 67: *K13, k2tog; rep from * to end (56 sts)

Row 68: *K12, k2tog; rep from * to end (52 sts)

Row 69: *K11, k2tog; rep from * to end (48 sts)

Row 70: *K2, k2tog; rep from* to end (36 sts)

Row 71 – 76: K to end

Row 77:  *K2, inc 1; rep from * to end (48 sts)

Row 78: *K11, inc 1; rep from * to end (52 sts)

Row 79: *K12, inc 1; rep from * to end (56 sts)

Row 80: *K13, inc 1; rep from * to end (60 sts)

Row 81: *K14, inc 1; rep from * to end, (64 sts)

Row 82 – 65: K to end

Row 83: *K14, k2tog; rep from * to end, (60sts)

Row 84: *K13, k2tog; rep from * to end (56 sts)

Row 85: *K12, k2tog; rep from * to end (52 sts)

Row 86: *K11, k2tog; rep from * to end (48 sts)

Row 87: *K10, k2tog; rep from * to end (44 sts)

Row 88 – 104, (all even rows): *K to end

Row 89: *K9, k2tog; rep from * to end (40 sts)

Row 91: *K8, k2tog; rep from * to end (36 sts)

Row 93: *K7, k2tog; rep from * to end (32 sts)

Row 95: *K6, k2tog; rep from * to end (28 sts)

Row 97: *K5, k2tog; rep from * to end (24 sts)

Row 99: *K4, k2tog; rep from * to end (20 sts)

Row 101: *K3, k2tog; rep from * to end (16 sts)

Row 103: *K2, k2tog; rep from * to end (14 sts)

Cut yarn leaving an 18-inch tail. Thread needle with yarn tail, pull through remaining stitches

# Mr. Snow's Hat

NOTE: I have found that not all wools, claiming to be 100% wool, will felt. Save precious time, frustration and money. Buy your wool through a knitting shop. Ask them which wools felt up well. Trust me, it is worth it!

## MATERIALS

- Double Pointed Needles US #11 / 8.0mm
- Yarn: 1 Skein, Lamb's Pride
  Worsted 85% Wool/15%Mohair
  4oz. (113 Grams) 190 yards

Gauge: 3" = 8 stitches; 3" = 10 rows vertical

## MAKING THE HAT

**Cast on 110 stitches onto dpn's, divide evenly between 4 needles**

Row 1: *K8, k2tog; rep from * to end

Row 2: K to end

Row 3: K5, *k2tog, k8; rep from * to end k2

Row 4: K to end

Row 5: K2,*k2 tog, k8; rep from * to end, k5 (80 sts)

Row 6: K to end

Row 7: *K6, k2tog; rep from * to end

Row 8-25: K to end

Row 26: P to end (70 sts)

Row 27 *K8, k2tog; rep from * to end (63 sts)

Row 28-29: K to end

Row 30: K2tog, *k12, k2 tog; rep from * to end, k2 tog, k4

Row 31: K4 *k2tog, k12; rep from * to end, k2 tog, k9 (53 sts)

Row 32-33: K to end

Row 34: K2, k2tog*k5 k2tog; rep from * to end (45 sts)

Row 35: K to end

Row 36: *K4, k2tog; rep from * to end, k3 (38 sts)

Row 37: K to end

Row 38: *K2tog, k4; rep from * to end, k2tog (31 sts)

Row 39: *K2tog, k4; rep from * to end k2tog (24 sts)

Row 40: *K2tog, k2; rep from * to end (20 sts)

Row 41: K to end

Row 42: *K2, k2tog rep from * to end (14 sts)

Row 43: *K1, k2tog; rep from * to end, k2 (10 sts)

Draw string through rem sts, fasten ends in.

## FELTING

- 22 sts = 6"h, after felting 4"h
- 20sts = 7"w, after felting 6"w

Wash in hot water with a pair of jeans and detergent. I took a wire hanger and formed it into a circle (8" dia.), wove it through the edge of the hat, then bent the ends to make it stay circular. Cut strip of fairly thin cardboard 5" wide x 20" long. Connect the ends with binder clips to form a cylinder. Pin to hat to form hat. Dry in clothes dryer. Check periodically to make sure it isn't felting too fast. Continue process and repeat until desired results.

## RED HAT BAND

Cast on 5 sts knit in stockinette stitch, (with the same yarn that you will use for the bow tie) until trim piece fits around hat. Sew ends together, careful not to twist. Tack onto hat.

# Mr. Snow's Vest

NOTE: Increases are made by knitting into the front and back of the stitch.

## MATERIALS

- Needles US #7 / 4.5mm
- Yarn: 100% Natural Alpaca Weight
  3 ply 5 oz. 604 yds,
  Gauge: 4" = 13 rows; 4" = 13 sts.

## MAKING THE VEST

### BACK
**Cast on 40 sts**

Row 1: *K1, p1; rep from*
Row 2: *P1, k1; rep from*
Row 3: *K1, p1; rep from*
Row 4: K to end
Row 5: P to end
Repeat rows 4 & 5 until piece measures 4" end on k row

*Begin Armholes*

Row 1: B.O. 3 sts, P to end
Row 2: B.O. 3 sts, K to end
Row 3: P2tog, p to end
Row 4: K2tog, k to end
Row 5: P2tog, p to end
Row 6: K2tog, k to end
Row 7: P2tog, p to end

Row 8: K2tog, k to end (28 sts)
Row 9: P to end
Row 10: K to end
Row 11: P to end
Row 12: K to end
Row 13: P to end
Row 14: K to end
Row 15: Inc1, *k1, p1; rep from * to end inc1
Row 16: *K1, p1; rep from * to end
Row 17: *P1, k1; rep from * to end
B.O. in pattern

### LEFT FRONT
**Cast on 20 sts**

Row 1: *P1, k1; rep from * to end
Row 2: *P1, k1; rep from * to end
Row 3: *P1, k1; rep from * to end
Row 4: K to end

Row 5: P to end

Row 6 – 11: Repeat row 4 & 5

Row 12: *K2tog, k1; rep from * to end

Row 13: P to end

Row 14: *k2tog, k1; rep from * to end

Row 15: P to end

Row 16: *K2tog, k1; rep from * to end

Row 17: BO 3 sts, p to end (14 sts)

Row 18: K2tog, k to end

Row 19: P2tog, p to end

Row 20 – 24: Rep rows 18 & 19

Row 25: P to end

Row 26 & 28: K to end

Row 27 & 29: P to end

Row 30: *P1, k1; rep from * to end

Row 31: *K1, p1; rep from * to end

Row 32: *P1, k1; rep from * to end

B.O. in pattern

**Using yarn A and yarn B held together:**
**Cast on 30 sts loosely**

## RIGHT FRONT
Cast on 20 sts

Row 1: *P1, k1; rep from * to end

Row 2: *P1, k1; rep from * to end

Row 3: *P1, k1; rep from * to end

Row 4: K to end

Row 5: P to end

Row 6 – 11: Rep row 4 & 5

Row 12, 14, 16: K until last 2 sts, k2tog

Row 13, 15, 17: P to end

Row 18: BO 3 sts, k to last 2 sts, k2tog

Row 19: P to last 2 sts, p2tog

Row 20: K until last 2 sts, k2tog

Row 21 – 24: Repeat rows 19 & 20

Row 25, 27, 29: P to end

Row 26 & 28: K to end

Row 30: *P1, k1; rep from * to end

Row 31: *K1, p1; rep from * to end

Row 32: *P1, k1; rep from * to end

B.O. in pattern

## LEFT FRONT TRIM
**Pick up 29 sts from the bottom to the top**
**along vest edge.**

Row 1: *P1, k1; rep from * to end

Row 2: *K1, p1; rep from * to end

Row 3: *P1, k1; rep from * to end

Rep for right front trim

BO in pattern

## RIGHT FRONT TRIM
**Pick up 29 sts from the bottom to the top along vest edge.**

Row 1: *K1, p1; rep from * to end

Row 2: *P1, k1; rep from * to end

Row 3: *K1, p1; rep from * to end

BO in pattern

# Nose Pattern

## MATERIALS

- Double Pointed Needles: US# 4 / 3.5mm

- Orange Worsted Weight Yarn

## MAKING THE NOSE

**Cast on 12 divide onto 3 dpn's**

Rows 1 – 10: K to end

Row 11: *K2tog, k2; rep from * to end

Row 12 – 15: K to end

Row 16: *K2tog, k1; rep from * to end

Row 17 & 18: K to end

Row 19: K2 tog to end onto 1 needle

Pull 1 over the next, casting off

• • •

# Mr. Snow's Tie

NOTE: Increases are made by knitting into the front and back of the stitch.

## MATERIALS

*   **Worsted Weight Yarn**

    **Needles: US # 6 / 4.0mm**

## MAKING THE TIE

**Cast on 4 sts**

Row 1 – 5: K all odd rows, p all even rows

Row 6: Inc1, p2, inc 1

Row 7: K to end

Row 8 – 13: repeat rows 6 & 7 (12 sts)

Row 14 – 22: P all even rows, k all odd rows

Row 23: k2tog, k8, k2tog

Row 24: P to end

Row 25 – 30: repeat Row 23 & 24 (4 sts)

Row 31 – 35: K, all odd rows, P all even rows

Row 36: Inc 1, p2, inc1 (6 sts)

Row 37: K to end

Row 38 – 42: repeat rows 36 & 37

Row 43 – 52: K all odd rows, P all even rows

Row 53: K2tog, k8, k2tog (10 sts)

Row 54: P to end

Row 55 – 59: repeat Rows 53 & 54 (4 sts)

Row 60: P to end

Row 61: K to end

B.O.

**Cast on 8 sts**

Stockinette stitch until 3"

Bind off

Sew bowtie together and sew middle piece around it.

Sew onto Snowman.

# Mrs. Snow's Scarf

NOTE: Increases are made by knitting into the front and back of the stitch.

## MATERIALS

- Needles: US #10 / 6.0mm
- 2 Skeins Loops and Threads Dewdrops Super Bulky #6, Color #5 Amethyst 71 yds/65m, net wt 3 oz, Color #5 Amethyst 51% Acrylic, 18% Mohair, 18% Polyamide, 8 % Polyester/ 5% Payette

## MAKING THE SCARF

Cast on 15 sts onto straight needles

Row 1 (right side): K2, *yf, sl 1, k2tog, psso, yf, k1; rep from * to last st, k1

Row 2: P to end

Row 3: K1, k2tog, yf, k1, *yf, sl 1, k2tog, psso, yf, k1; rep from* to last 3 sts, yf, sl 1, k1, psso, k1

Row 4: P to end

Repeat 4 rows until piece measures approximately 4' – 6" or you are at the end of the skein.

• • •

# Mrs. Snow's Hat

NOTE: Increases are made by knitting into the front and back of the stitch.
Size- Adult Small/Child Medium

## MATERIALS

- 2 Skeins Loops and Threads Dewdrops Super Bulky #6, 71 yds/65m, net wt 3 oz, Color #5 Amethyst 51%Acrylic, 18% Mohair, 18% Polyamide, 8 % Polyester/ 5% Payette
- Straight Needles US #10 / 6.0mm
- Double Pointed Needles US #10 / 6.0mm
- Circular Needles US #10 / 6.0mm

  Gauge: 5 sts = 2"; 7 rows

## MAKING OF THE HAT

### BAND
Cast on 14 sts onto straight needles

Row 1: K2, p1, c4b, k2, k2, p1, k2
Row 2: P2, k1, p8, k1, p2
Row 3: K2, p1, k2, c4f, p1, k2
Row 4: P2, k1, p8, k1, p2
Repeat rows 1 – 4 until piece measures 23" Sew hat band ends together, making sure not to twist the band.

### TOP OF HAT
Pick up 62 sts along the edge of the band onto a circular needle, changing to dpn's when necessary.

Row 1: K1, *yf, sl 1, k2tog, psso, yf, k1; rep from * to last st k1
Row 2: K to end
Row 3: K1, k2tog, yf, k1, *yf, sl 1, k2tog, psso, yf, k1; rep from * to last 3 sts, yf, sl 1, k1, psso, k1
Row 4: K to end
Row 5: K2tog, k1, *yf, sl 1, k2tog, psso, yf, k1; rep from * 7 times, k2tog, *sl 1, k2tog, psso, yf, k1; rep from * to last st, k1
Row 6: *K2tog, k8; rep from * to end
Row 7: K2tog, k2tog, yf, k1, *yf, sl 1, k2tog, psso, yf, k1; rep from * to end
Row 8: *K2tog, k6; rep from * to end
Row 9: K2tog, k1, *yf, sl 1, k2tog, psso, yf, k1; rep from * to end k1
Row 10: *K2tog, k4; rep from * to end
Row 11: *K2tog, k2tog, yf, k1; rep from * to end

Row 12: *K2tog, k2; rep from * to end
Row 13: *K2tog, k1; rep from * to end
Row 14: K2tog to end (6s ts)

Cut yarn leaving a 6-inch tail. Thread needle with yarn tail, pull through remaining stitches.

### FLOWER
Cast on 5 sts

Knit stockinette st until piece is long enough to make a flower with 5 petals. Make flower approx 3" wide. Sew together. Sew onto pin or sew onto hat.

# Assembly of Mr. and Mrs. Snow

## MATERIALS

- 3 Styrofoam balls: 1 - 10" ball 25.4cm; Two 8" ball 20.3 cm
- 5/16" x 36" Dowel – Make sure it fits into the bushing
- ¾" x 3/8" Galvanized Hex Bushing
- 3/8" x 1/8" Galvanized Hex Bushing
- ¾" NPT flange 3-1/2" diameter
- Hot glue gun
- Measuring tape or ruler
- Box Cutter
- 3" & 4" diameter bowl or glass to trace onto balls
- Serrated large bread knife
- Candle

Assemble Hardware (Screw ¾" x 3/8" hex bushing into the flange, then screw the 3/8" x 1/8" hex bushing into the ¾ x 3/8" bushing. Hot glue dowel into bushing.

Cut dowel to 19" whittle tip to point with box cutter. Insert flat end of dowel into the hex bushing.

Trace 3" onto 10" Styrofoam ball

Slide knife through unlit candle to wax it

Cut on traced lines by rotating ball

Trace 4 1/2" on top of other side of the 10" ball (this is the bottom of snow person)

Stand back and walk around to make sure it's straight, Cut same as above.

Trace the 3" circle onto the top and bottom of one 8" ball, for the body and cut with waxed knife.

Trace the 3" circle onto one side of one 8" ball for the head and cut with waxed knife

Put dowel apparatus on ground. Mark center of the bottom of the 10" ball. Make sure 4" cut is on the bottom and begin to push onto dowel. Next push the middle ball on top and then push the head on top.

Use body weight to push the snow person all the way down over the bushings. Finally put the snow person's "skin" on.

2 branches, slip knot onto branch and begin to wind yarn around the branch. Sew end in and put a dot of glue (any glue, tacky, hot glue) on ends, to make sure that the yarn is secure. Admire your work!

• • •

# Vine Runner Décor

• • •

*Fanciful garland, composed of imaginary leaves, comes alive in a fantastic presentation on a table or a gorgeous array on a mantel. Display it on top of an armoire, adding twinkle lights for atmosphere. Adorn the space above your door openings with this lovely festoon. You will find many uses for this simple yet beautiful garland.*

• • •

Great project to use up your left-over wool! Your garland can incorporate anything you want. Perfect for a beautiful winter garland or fashion a sumptuous autumn piece in crimsons, apricots, cocoas, and shades of honey. Imagination being limitless, this particular project beckons its creator to push the envelope and fabricate something spectacular.

# Vine Décor

NOTE: Increases are made by knitting into the front and back of the stitch. I have found that not all wools, claiming to be 100% wool, will felt. Save precious time, frustration and money. Buy your wool through a knitting shop. Ask them which wools felt up well. Trust me, it is worth it!

## MATERIALS

- **Natural Color Felting Wool**
- **Red Felting Wool**
- **Green Felting Wool**

   **22 Gauge Wire (or less, which is thicker wire)**

Cast on 6 sts:

Knit I cord for 9' (this will give you an approx 6' finished cord), bind off and fasten ends in. Guide wire through cord, loop wire ends and twist. Cast on 5 sts and knit I cord for 5", bind off, sew one end in and with other end sew onto the long I cord, fairly even distances apart. Make approx 9 – 5" cords. Slide wire through and twist onto the main wire. Leave the wire on the branches stick out about an inch, so that you may add the leaves on later. You will still want to tack them down with thread, but they will be bendable and easier to manipulate into a display. Coil up loosely and follow felting process.

Using red yarn cast on 60 sts, K until piece is 30" long. Follow felting process in Stitch Glossary. Using green yarn rep

Draw pattern or copy from book and cut out leaves. Using similar colored thread, sew leaves onto vine. Feel free to experiment with your own ideas. Add more leaves, add different colors. Make an autumn vine, or a springtime pastel vine. Cut to suit your needs. Let your imagination run wild.

# Design Tip: DECORATING THE CHRISTMAS TREE

Things to keep in mind when designing your tree: Color, balance, flow, texture, contrast and composition. If you get stuck, think of the perfection nature offers and try to reproduce the beauty we find outdoors.

Trees, like anything else you are designing need to have some reoccurring elements. Choose ribbon to wrap in and out of your tree or similar ornaments, bows, or a color that you will repeat throughout the tree and your room. This will tie everything together. Trees need to be balanced and color can help to achieve this. Color does not need to be distributed evenly throughout the tree. In fact, the tree will be more interesting if you mix it up a bit. Produce a symphony of color! Use a color more in a few areas and accents of color here and there. This way your eye will move around the tree and discover all the treasures it has to offer. Using too many colors can cause visual chaos, so stick to 3 to 5 major colors. Play Christmas music while decorating your tree for inspiration.

Your tree is a new element in your space. If you have room, by all means pull it out from the wall. There is no rule to keep your tree held hostage against the wall. Consider that your tree is a very natural object in the room and a large one at that. It is meant to be the focal point, yet the room should be visually balanced with some sort of furniture, color and texture opposing the tree. The tree is multi-dimensional, as it is a focal point onto itself and within the composition of the tree are mini focal points, which is what makes a tree so fascinating to take in.

# Angel

• • •

*Modern times are hectic; making it obvious that time is our most valuable resource. Heartfelt thanks of the sincerest nature are given when a handmade gift is exchanged. Angels are the ultimate symbol embodying care and love. Present the gift of love in this glorious present.*

• • •

You will want to make several of these to give to family and friends. Teachers and co-workers will be seriously humbled if they are lucky enough to receive an angel. This is my favorite gift to throw around the neck of a bottle of wine and give as a hostess gift. Each angel tends to be born with their own personality which makes them fun to create and watch as they come to life.

# Angel

NOTE: Making an I cord: K across row, do not turn work, but slide it to the other side of the needle and begin to knit with the yarn that is now on the left hand side of the work. It seems wrong, but pull it taut and knit that row. Once again, do not turn your work, but slide it the other side of the needle and repeat.

## MATERIALS

- Set of 5 Double Pointed Needles US #3 / 2.5mm
- 1 Skein - White Acrylic Light Worsted Weight Yarn
- 1 Skein – Sport Weight, Baby Yarn, 96% Acrylic, 4% Metallic Polyester, (Vanna's Glamour) Gauge 1" = 5 stitches; 1" = 6 rows

## MAKING THE ANGEL BODY

**Cast on 72 St. evenly on dpn's (24 sts each needle)**

Row 1: *P9, k3; rep from * to end

Row 2: *P9, k3; rep from * to end

Row 3: *Spp, p5, p2tog, k3; rep from * to end

Row 4: *P7, k3; rep from * to end

Row 5: *Spp, p3, p2 tog, k3; rep from * to end

Row 6: *P5, k3; rep from * to end

Row 7: *Spp, p1, p2 tog, k3; rep from * to end

Row 8: *P3, kp3; rep from * to end

Row 9: *Sp2p, k3; rep from * to end

Row 10: *P2, k3 rep; from * to end

Row 11: *P2 tog, k3; rep from * to end

Row 12: *P1, k3; rep from * to end

Row 13: *P2, k2; tog rep from * to end, k1

Row 14: *P1, k3; rep from * to end

Row 15: *P1, k2 tog; rep from * to end

Row 16 - 20: *P1, k1; rep from * to end

Row 21 - 23: K to end

Row 24: *K2 tog rep from*

Row 25 & 26: K to end

*Begin Head*

Row 27: Inc 1 all stitches

Row 28, 30, 32, 34, 36: K to end

Row 29: *K2, inc 1; rep from * to end

Row 31: *Inc 1, k2; rep from * to end

Row 33: *K2, k2tog; rep from * to end, k1

Row 35: K2tog, end k1

Roll yarn into a ball, stuff into the head. Thread needle, pull through stitches and fasten.

## ARMS & HALO

Cast on 3 sts with silver yarn (work as I cord, see instructions above in NOTES) the piece measures (6" in white for arms and 3-3/4" for halo), then bind off. Sew arms onto back of Angel under the head. Arrange arms into prayer position and sew hands together. Sew halo onto back/top of head.

## WING 1

**Cast on 22 sts**

Row 1 and every odd row: K to end
Row 2: *K2, yo, k1, k2tog; rep from * to end k2
Row 4: *K1, yo, k1, k2tog; rep from * to end k1, yo, k1
Row 6: *K1, yo, k1, k2tog; rep from * to end k1, yo, k2
Row 8: *K2, yo, k1, k2tog; rep from * to end k2, yo, k2
Row 10: *K1, yo, k1, k2tog; rep from * to end k1

Row 12: *K2, yo, k1, k2tog; rep from *
Row 14: *K1, yo, k1, k2tog; rep from * end k1
Row 15: B.O.

## WING 2

**Cast on 22 sts**

Row 1 and every odd row: P to end
Row 2: *P2, yo, p1, p2tog; rep from * to end p2
Row 4: *P1, yo, p1, p2tog; rep from * to end p1, yo, p1
Row 6: *P1, yo, p1, p2tog; rep from * to end p1, yo, p2
Row 8: *P2, yo, p1, p2tog; rep from * to end p2, yo, p2
Row 10: *P1, yo, p1, p2tog; rep from * to end p1
Row 12: *P2, yo, p1, p2tog; rep from * to end
Row 14: *P1, yo, p1, p2tog; rep from * to end p1
Row 15: B.O.

Sew onto back of angel to form wings

# Tree Skirt

• • •

*This flirty skirt wraps luxuriously around your tree in a soft, bulky textured yarn, reminiscent of trees, blanketed with snow, after the first big storm of the season. Bright white this extravagant skirt has a distinct glimmer quality. The vision of snowy drifts hugging your tree couldn't be truer, unless your Christmas tree was left uncut in nature. This yarn is so soft and skirt so fabulous, that you may want to use it to wrap around yourself instead of your tree. Ah, the little luxuries of life. Treat yourself to this decadent tree skirt and every year, as you bring it out, a sense of pride overtakes you as you wrap this lovely skirt around your tree, taking your tree from beautiful to extraordinary. You might just want to hike your tree up so that everyone can see your skirt!*

• • •

This skirt is made on circular needles, but is not knit in rounds, instead is knit back and forth similar to straight needles. The circular needle is used to hold the tremendous amount of stitches needed to make this piece. Another interesting thing to note is that there is no sewing up, except for ends, which makes this a perfect project for those who despise this part of the process.

# Tree Skirt

NOTE: Increases are made by knitting into the front and back of the stitch.

## MATERIALS

- Needles: 2) Circular US #10 / 6.0mm, 60"
- 5 Skeins Loops and Thread Charisma yarn, 109yds/100m, Net wt 3.5 oz, 100% Acrylic, Bulky #5

## MAKING THE TREE SKIRT

**Cast on 50 sts**

Row 1 and every odd row unless otherwise noted: K to end

Row 2: *P8, inc1; rep from * to end p5

Row 4: P2, inc1, *p8, inc1; rep from * to end p7

Row 6: P7, inc1, *p10, inc1; rep from * to end p9

Row 8: P5, inc1, *p10, inc1; rep from * to end p5

Row 10: *P12, inc1; rep from * to end p7

Row 12: P to end

Row 13: P3, inc1, *p12, inc1; rep from * to end p8

Row 14: K to end

Row 15: *P12, inc1; rep from * to end p5

Row 16: K to end

Row 17: Inc1 every st knitting purlwise

## START 1ST RUFFLE

Row 1: *K1, put the next stitch onto another circular needle; rep from * to end, place point protectors on ends so that the stitches don't fall off. Begin to knit with one of the circular needles.

Row 2: P to end

Row 4: *P15, inc 1; rep from * to end p9

Row 6: P6, inc 1, *p15, inc1; rep from * to end p7

Row 8: *K1, inc 1; rep from * to end

Row 10: *P, inc 1; rep from * to end

B.O.

## BODY OF SKIRT

Row 18: Attach yarn to other circular needle and p to end

Row 20: P15, inc 1, *p15, inc 1; rep from * to end p9

Row 22: P6, inc 1, *p15, inc 1; rep from * to end p7

Row 24: P3, inc 1, *p15, inc 1; rep from * to end p1

Row 26: *P15, inc 1; rep from * to end p10

Row 28: P8, inc 1, *p15, inc 1; rep from * to end p7

Row 30: *P15, inc 1; rep from * to end p7

Row 32: P5, inc 1, *p15, inc 1; rep from * to end p8

Row 34: *P15, inc 1; rep from * to end p6

Row 36: P3, inc 1, *p15, inc 1; rep from * to end p10

Row 38: *P15, inc 1; rep from * to end p7

Row 40: P7, inc 1, *p15, inc 1; rep from * to end p8

Row 42: P5, inc 1, *P15, inc 1; rep from* to end p4

Row 44: Inc 1 in every st knitting purlwise

*Start 2nd ruffle*

Row 1: *K1, put one on another circular needle; rep from * to end, place point protectors on ends so that the stitches don't fall off.  Begin to knit with one of the circular needles.

Row 2: P to end

Row 4: *P15, inc 1; rep from * to end p5

Row 6: P6, inc 1, *P15, inc 1; rep from * to end p7

Row 8: *K1, inc 1; rep from * to end

Row 10: *P1, inc 1; rep from * to end

B.O.

## BODY OF SKIRT AND 3RD RUFFLE

Row 45: Attach yarn to circular needle and K to end

Row 46: *P15, inc 1; rep from * to end p15

Row 48: P6, inc 1, *p15, inc 1; rep from

* to end p9

Row 50: P3, inc 1, *p15, inc 1; rep from * to end p13

Row 52: *P15, inc 1; rep from * to end p9

Row 54: P6, inc 1, *p15, inc 1; rep from * to end p15

Row 56: *P15, inc 1; rep from * to end p4

Row 58: P3, inc 1, *p15, inc 1; rep from * to end p15

Row 60: *P15, inc 1; rep from * to end p8

Row 62: *P15, inc 1; rep from * to end p4

Row 64: P3, inc 1, *p15, inc 1; rep from * to end p2

Row 66: P5, inc 1, *p15, inc 1; rep from * to end p4

Row 68: *K1, inc 1; rep from * to end

Row 69: *P1, inc 1; rep from * to end

BO

Sew in loose ends

# Advent Calendar/
# Card Holder

• • •

*The mountain lodge is rustic, the Christmas old-fashioned, snow is blowing, the fire
is roaring as anticipation rises for the festive day full of surprises. Year after year of
repeating the same customs, a tradition is made. This functional advent calendar is
hung, tempting the kids to open all the adorable little pouches and reveal the goodies!
Cards are clipped on as they come in, onto metal clips that replace the pouches that
have served their purpose. These are the memories that are etched in our minds
for a lifetime.*

• • •

A project that has the potential for generating memories that make our children's holidays special is
worth a little time and effort. The calendar incorporates a few crafty disciplines. You will need your sewing machine, needles and thread, washing machine, possibly a hand saw, as well as your knitting needles
and yarn. It is worth all of this for the huge joy this will bring your loved ones. Follow one step at a
time and before you know it, you will have an incredible piece that will be enjoyed for years to come and
help build family tradition. Enjoy this calendar as another excellent project to use up leftover yarn.

# Advent Calendar/ Card Holder

NOTE: Increases are made by knitting into the front and back of the stitch. I have found that not all wools, claiming to be 100% wool, will felt. Save precious time, frustration and money. Buy your wool through a knitting shop. Ask them which wools felt up well. Trust me, it is worth it!

Because this piece is so long I used two pillow cases tied together for the process

MATERIALS

- Needles: US #10 / 6.0mm
- Yarn: Choose 2 colors for the base. Choose 5 accent colors for the satchels. Shown as foll:
- Lion Brand Fisherman's wool, 1 Skein, 100% Virgin Wool, Bulk #4, 8 oz. / 465 yds, Color Oatmeal, or any felting wool that is a natural color
- Dark Green Felting Wool: 1 Skein – New Zealand Wool Wellington, 100% Perendale Super Wool, Color 096 Green Heather
- Dark Red Felting Wool: 2 Skeins - Lambs Pride, 85% Wool, 15% Mohair, Worsted Weight, 190 yds Color: M-83
- Five Coordinating Colors for Satchels: 1 Skein Each – Bernat, Roving, 80 % Acrylic, 20% Wool, Colors: Bark, Rice Paper, Low Tide

- Lion Brand, 1 Skein Each - Wool-Ease, worsted weight, Colors: 174 Avocado, 107 Blue Heather
- Checkheaton Country, 1 Skein – 12 Ply, 100% Pure Wool, Color 18 (Dk. Red), 78 yds/ 71 metres
- 3/4" Hole Punch
- 24 Buttons, at least 1" diameter
- 24 Snaps
- Findings Jewelry Essentials Alligator Clips
- Findings Jewelry Essentials Large Wire Hoop Assortment
- Coordinating thread to sew on snaps
- Thick branch or dowel for hanging calendar Gauge: 2" = 7 rows; 2" = 6 sts

## MAKING THE CALENDAR/HOLDER

CO 62 sts with natural wool (Fisherman's Wool)
K until skein is gone or piece is approx 52 - 57" long
or until skein is used up.

CO 20 sts with dark red felting wool, (Lamb's Pride)
Knit until piece is approx 4'-6" long
Foll felting process

## TREES

C.0. 60 sts

K till approx 12".

Foll felting process above, cut trees from template in
the back of this book or create your own design

## SATCHELS

C.0. 14 sts

Make 24 satchels. Experiment with different color
combinations within the 5 chosen colors. Begin to
double knit.

Row 1 & 2:  *p1, sl 1; rep from * to end

Row 3, 5, 7 & 13:  Attach blue yarn *k1, (yarn in
front), sl 1 as if to p, (yarn in back) k1; rep from
* to end

Row 4, 6, 8, 10, 12 & 14: *P1, sl 1; rep from * to end

Row 9: Add red, rep row 3

Row 11: Add blue green, rep row3

Row 15: *K1, (yarn in front), sl 1 onto other needle
or holder, (yarn in back), k1, bo; rep from * to end

Row 16 : Add blue, k sts from holder to end

Row 17: *K; rep from * to end

Row 18 & 20: *P; rep from * to end

Row 19: *K; rep from * to end

Row 21: Add red, *k; rep from * to end

B.0.

Make a handle for satchel, chain st about 3" long

Fasten in ends, sew on snaps.

For card holder take large hoops, bend end with
needle nose pliers so that it is at a right angle to the
circle.  Put through the alligator clip.  Hook over button and you are ready to display cards.

# Festive Holiday
# Ball Décor

• • •

Balls to the walls!  Or better yet, balls away from the walls.  Fuzzy, bursts of fun appear to float in mid air.  Simple balls, amazingly and almost independently, invoke the magic of the holidays.  Unbelievably diverse in arrangement and configuration, they truly are; Balls of Wonder.

• • •

This is a fast, simple project that brings immediate gratification to the knitter.  Make a few or make a bunch and every year, your creative juices will flow using them in your space any which way your imagination can conjure up.

# Festive Holiday Ball Decor

NOTE: Instruction for 5", 4", 3" and 2" balls. Increases are made by knitting into the front and back of the stitch.

## MATERIALS

- Needles: Set of 5 US #4 / 3.5mm
- Yarns: Worsted Weight 4 Ply and Lion Brand Fun Fur of the same color
- Stitch marker
- 2", 3", 4" and/or 5" Styrofoam Ball(s)

## MAKING THE HOLIDAY BALLS

Cast on 6 sts, divide sts equally among 3 dpn's, place stitch marker and begin to knit in the round, add a 4th needle as needed.

Row 1: K

Row 2: *Inc 1; rep from* to end (12 sts)

Row 3 and all odd rows: Knit to end

Row 4: *K1, Inc 1; rep from * to end (18 sts)

Row 6: *K2, Inc 1; rep from * to end (24 sts)

For 2" ball skip to Row 26 and continue to end

Row 8: *K3, Inc 1; rep from * to end (30 sts)

Row 9: *K4, Inc 1; rep from * to end (36 sts)

For 3" ball skip to Row 22 and continue to end

Row 10: *K5, Inc 1; rep from * to end (42 sts)

Row 12: *K6, Inc 1; rep from * to end (48 sts)

For 4" ball skip to Row 18 and continue to end

Row 14: *K7, Inc 1; rep from * to end (54 sts)

Row 16: *K7, k2tog; rep from * to end (48 sts)

Row 18: *K6, k2tog; rep from * to end (42 sts)

Row 20: *K5, k2tog; rep from * to end (36 sts)

Row 22: *K4, k2tog; rep from * to end (30 sts)

Row 24: *K3, k2tog; rep from * to end (24 sts)

Row 26: *K2, k2tog; rep from * to end (18 sts)

Insert Styrofoam Ball

Row 28: *K1, k2tog; repeat from * to end (12 sts)

Row 30: *K2tog; repeat from * to end (6 sts)

Row 31: K to end

Cut yarn leaving a 6-inch tail. Thread needle with yarn tail, pull through remaining stitches and sew ends in. Snip excess tail close to ball's surface. Makes an approximate 5-inch diameter ball Attach a nylon thread if you wish to hang the ball.

• • •

# Design Tip: DISPLAYS

Use them to create a lively entryway display or to embellish a festive dining table environment.  Add these balls to any area to help create a whimsical, fantastical element to your holiday décor.

Suspended in mid air at differing heights, the balls create playful, visual movement.  A display of these balls instantly reminds you that these are special times filled with merriment.

Hang them at differing levels, allowing your eye to move around the space and create a sense of motion.  Hanging them with a spattering of different sizes will add spatial depth, giving you a slight sense of vertigo that ignites excitement.  Placing them at various depths will add dimension to the space.  Hang them over a piece of furniture, such as a table, piano or island, high enough off the floor so that people will not bump into them.

Artistically hung onto a branch over a dining table makes for memorable and enchanting décor.  However you choose to decorate with these balls, it is guaranteed to instantly make you aware that it is time for celebration.  Arranging them down the center of a dining room table, as part of a centerpiece with greens and candles, promises a romantic dining experience.  Place them in a hurricane lamp to add color, texture and softness to an area.  Hang them from your Christmas tree to add softness and texture.   Make them in black and white for your New Years Eve party.

One of the most common design mistakes is to forget to address the ceiling.  When everything is placed at three feet to five feet around the room, that is where you eye stays and this type of arrangement tends to be bland.  When you have something such as these versatile balls in your arsenal, it is easy to create real drama, drawing your eye up and around a room.  Remember to balance out the space with something of the same color or texture (such as the dot pillows) on the opposing side of the room.  Color and texture this is an element that can add to the cohesiveness of your room design.  These balls add movement to a space, while evoking excitement and drama.

# Stockings

• • •

*Hanging stockings by the chimney, with anticipation that something miraculous will happen epitomizes what Christmas is all about.  Miracles transpire around us.*

*Stockings represent the gift of giving and receiving that excites our souls.  Rewards for our hearts are grand when we are able to give.  We are blessed beyond this when we are lucky enough to feel the gratefulness from the receiver, for our intentions.  It makes us feel loved and special.*

• • •

Dreams really do come true when a child receives one of these generously oversized stockings! Measuring in at about two feet long, they are absolutely extravagant with two exquisite patterns to choose from.

# Design Tip: STOCKINGS

Which is the "right" way to point the toes? According to my research, I have found that most of the time the toes point to the (drum roll please) the right. In my humble opinion, I don't think it matters a bit, except for a couple things.

One is that in the future, you may want to add different stockings and if you are adding stockings that are unlike each other, you will want them to face the same way, so that they have something in common. Number two is that when adding stockings that are toe to toe, you will not be able to fit as many on your mantle. Aesthetically, it depends on many things to determine which way to go on this dilemma. Things to consider; are the stockings of similar color and texture, size and shape? If so, then you could hang them mirrored image, meaning toes pointing toward each other or away from each other and this would be just as "right" as hanging them all with the toes pointing in the same direction.

If they are not the same, but have some similarities, (such as the two different patterns submitted in this book), the former rule also holds true, but make sure you have the same number of stockings on each side.  Basically, in order to hang stockings in opposing directions, they need to have some things in common, size, color, shape or texture and number of socks.

## BREAKING THE RULE

Symmetry is the goal in the stocking hanging world.  Bend this rule here and there, as long as there are common threads to carry out the composition successfully, and then my friend, you will be breaking the rule like a professional.

# Vine Stocking

NOTE:   Front Cable (FC)'s sl 1 st to cable needle (cn) and hold in front p1, then k1 from cb.  Front Knit Cable (FKC)'s same as FC, but knit both sts.  Front Purl Cable (FPC)'s same as FC, but purl both sts. Back Cable (BC)'s sl 1 st to cb and hold in back, k1, then p1 from cb.  Back Knit Cable (BKC)'s  same as BC, but knit both sts.  Back Purl Cable (BPC)'s same as BC, but purl both sts.

## MATERIALS

- 2 Skeins Bernat Roving Color: Rice Paper or any bulky #5 yarn

- 1 Skein Bernat Roving Color: Bark or any bulky #5 yarn

- Needles: US #10 / 6.0mm
  Gauge:  5 sts = 2"; 7 rows = 2"

## STOCKING CUFF
Cast on 18 sts

Row 1: (Right Side) – P2, k3, p3, k4, fkc, p4

Row 2: K3, fpc, p1, fc, p2, k3, bc, p1, k2

Row 3: P2, k2, p4, k2, p1, k3, fkc, p2

Row 4: K2, p3, fc, k1, p1, bpc, k3, bc, k2

Row 5: P6, bkc, k2, p2, k4, p2

Row 6: K2, p2, fc, k2, p1, bpc 2x k5

Row 7: P4, bkc, k4, p3, k3, p2

Row 8: K2, p1, fc, k3, p2, bc, p1, bpc, k3

Row 9: P2, bkc, k3, p1, k2, p4, k2, p2

Row 10: K2, fc, k3, fpc, p1, k1, bc, p3, k2

Row 11: P2, k4, p2, k2, fkc, p6

Row 12: K5, fpc, 2x, p1, k2, bc, p2, k2

Repeat Rows 1-12 until piece measures 18" or fits top of stocking.

## LEG
Cast on 50

Row 1: (Right Side) and all other odd rows - K to end

Row 2 & 6: K to end

Row 4: K1, *sl next 2 sts to dpn and hold in back, k2, k2 from dpn, k4; rep from * to end k1

Row 8: K1, *k4, sl next 2 sts to dpn and hold in front, k2, k2 from dpn; rep from * to end k1

Repeat Rows 1 - 8 until piece measures approximately 11 – ½"

## HEEL FLAP

Divide stitches for heel flap. Put 26 sts on one needle with tail being the end st so that you are ready to P the next row. Divide the remaining 24 sts in half so that you have 12 on one needle and 12 on the other. For the heel flap you will work the 26 sts only.

Row 1 and every odd row: S1, p to end
Row 2: S1, k to end
Row 4: S1, *next to st to cn and hold in back, k2, k2 from cn, k4; rep from * to end k1
Row 6: K to end
Row 8: S1, *k4, sl next 2 sts to cn and hold in front, k2, k2 from cn; rep from * to end k1
Repeat above

## HEEL TURN

Row 1: S1, p16, p2tog, p1, turn work
Row 2: S1, k9, ssk, k1, turn work
Row 3: S1, p10, p2tog, p1, turn work
Row 4: S1, k4, sl 2 sts to cn and hold in back, k2, k2 from cn, k3, ssk, k1, turn work
Row 5: S1, p12, p2tog, p1, turn work
Row 6: S1, k13, ssk, k1, turn work
Row 7: S1, p14, p2tog, p1, turn work
Row 8: S1, k4, sl 2 sts to cn and hold in front, k2, k2 from cn, k3, sl 2 sts to cn and hold in front, k2, k2 from cn, ssk, k1

Continue to Gusset pg. 46

## FLOWER APPLIQUÈ

Cast on 10 sts

Row 1: (Right Side) - K
Row 2: and all even rows - p
Row 3: *k into front and back of st; rep from * to end (20 sts)
Row 5: *K into front and back of sts; rep from * to end (40 sts)
Row 7: *K into front and back of sts; rep from * to end (80 sts)
B.O.

## CENTER OF FLOWER BOBBLE

Cast on 1 st

Row 1: K into front, back and front of st
Rows 2 - 6: K to end
Row 7: p3tog
Fasten off

*Tether with Bobble*

Chain st until piece measures 12"
MB - K in front, back front and back of st
K next 2 rows
K2tog twice
K2tog
Fasten
Repeat for two more tethers one measuring 10" and the other 7".

Sew flower, flower center and tethers onto the stocking.

● ● ●

## GUSSET

Round 1: Pick up 10 sts (previously sl sts along heel flap, k across front sts (k all 24 sts onto the same needle), pick up 11 sts along the other side of the heel flap on a new needle

Round 2: Needle one (heel): unless otherwise noted, K to end

Needle two: K1, k2tog, k to end

Needle three (front): unless otherwise noted, K to end

Needle four: K8, ssk, k1

Round 3:

Needle two: K1, k2tog, k6,

Needle four: K7, ssk, k1

Round 4: Needle one: K1, * sl 2 sts to cn and hold in back, k2, k2 from cn, k4, rep from* end k1,

Needle two: K1, k2tog, k5

Needle three: K1, sl 2 sts to cn and hold in back, k2, k2 from cn, k4 rep from* end k3

Needle four: K6, ssk, k1

Round 5: Needle two: K1, k2tog, k4,

Needle four: K5, ssk, k1

Round 6: Needle two: K1, k2tog, k3,

Needle four: K4, ssk, k1

Round 7: Needle two: k1, k2tog, k2

Needle four: K3, ssk, k1

Round 8: Needle one: *k4, sl 2 sts to cn and hold in front, k2, k2 from cn, rep from * to end k2

Needle two: Sl 2 sts to cn and hold in front, k2, k2 from cn

Needle three: *k4, sl 2 sts to cn and hold in front, k2, k2 from cn rep from*

Needle four: k2, ssk, k1

Round 9: Needle two: k to end

Needle four: Sl 2 sts to cn and hold in front, k2, k2 from cn

Rounds 10 & 11: K to end

Round 12: Needle one: k1, *sl 2 sts to cn and hold in back, k2, k2 from cn, k4, rep from * end k5,

Needle two: Sl 2 sts to cn and hold in back, k2, k2 from cn

Needle three: k1, * sl 2 sts to cn and hold in back, k2, k2 from cn, k4, rep from * to end k3

Needle four: Sl 2 sts to cn and hold in back, k2, k2 from cn

Round 13 - 15: K to end

Round 16: Needle one: *K4, sl 2 sts to cn and hold in front, k2, k2 from cn, rep from * to end k2

Needle two: Sl 2 sts to cn and hold in front, k2, k2 from cn

Needle three: *k4, sl 2 sts to cn and hold in front, k2, k2 from cn, rep from * to end

Needle four: K4

Rounds 17 – 19: K to end

• • •

Round 20: Needle one: k1, *sl 2 sts to cn and hold in back, k2, k2 from cn, k4, rep from * to end k1

Needle two: Sl 2 sts to cn and hold in back, k2, k2 from cn

Needle three: k1, *sl 2 sts to cn and hold in back, k2, k2 from cn, k4, rep from * to end

Needle four:  Sl 2 sts to cn and hold in back, k2, k2 from cn

Rounds 21 – 23: K to end

Round 24:  Needle one: *K4, sl 2 sts to cn and hold in front, k2, k2 from cn, rep from * to end k2

Needle two:  Sl 2 sts to cn and hold in front, k2, k2 from cn

Needle three: *K4, sl 2 sts to cn and hold in front, k2, k2 from cn, rep from* to end

Needle four: K4

Rounds 25 – 27: K to end

Divide heel and toe sts equally onto 2 needles (25 sts ea)

*Begin Toe*

Rounds 28 – 33: *K1, k2tog, k19, (17, 15, 13, 11, 9) ssk, k1; rep from * to end

Use Kitchener stitch to sew toe tip together.  Sew in ends and sew cuff to stocking.  Use chain stitch to make varied length decorations with a bobble end.  Bobble end:  K into the back, front, back, front, back of stitch, turn k all five stitches, turn and bind off.

# Ribbed Stocking

NOTE: Ssk: slip as if to k, slip as if to p, put left needle through the front of both sts and k. Bobble end: K into the back, front, back, front, back of stitch, turn k all five sts, turn and bind off. Increases are made by knitting into the front and back of the stitch.

## MATERIALS

- **Needles US #10 / 6.0mm**
- **Bernat Roving Color Rice Paper and Bark**
- **By - Brown yarn**

- **Wy -White yarn**

  Gauge: 6 sts; 2" 7 rows = 2"

## STOCKING CUFF
Cast on 42 sts by

Row 1 & 2: K to end

Row 3: P to end

Row 4 – 7: Wy, K to end

Row 8: By, k to end

Rows 9, 11, 13: P to end

Rows 10, 12: K to end

Row 14: Wy, K to end

Rows 15 – 17: K to end

Row 19: By, K to end

Row 20 – 22: P to end

Row 19 – 21: K to end

B.O.

## LEG
Cast on 56 on dp needles needle on 20sts, needle two 20 sts, needle three - 16 sts

Row 1, 2, 4: K1, *p2, k1, p2, k2, rep from* to end k1

Row 3: K1, *p2, mb, p2, k2, rep from* to end k1

Repeat till piece measures approx 12" ending after a 3rd row

## HEEL FLAP
Divide stitches for heel flap. Put 28 sts on one needle with tail being the end st so that you are ready to P the next row. Divide the remaining 24 sts in half so that you have 14 on one needle and 14 on the other. For the heel flap you will work the 28 sts only.

Row 1 & 3: (Wrong side) S1, k2, p1, k2, *p2, k2, p1, k2, rep from* to end p1

Row 2: S1, p2, k1, p2, *k2, p2, k1, p2, rep from * to end k1

Row 4: S1, p2, mb, p2, *k2, p2, mb, p2, rep from * to end k1

Repeat above 3 times ending after a Row 1.

## HEEL TURN

Row 1: S1, *p2, k1, p2, k2*; rep from* 2 times, p2, k1, p1, ssk, k1 turn work

Row 2: S1, p1, k1, p1, k2, p2, k2, p1, k1, p2tog, p1, turn work

Row 3: S1, k1, p1 mb, p2, k2, p2, mb, p1, k1, ssk, p1, turn work

Row 4: S1, p2, k1, p1, k2, p2, k2, p1, k1, p1, p2tog, k1, turn work

Row 5: S1, k2, p1, k1, p2, ,k2, p2, k1, p1, k2, ssk, p1, turn work

Row 6: S1, p3, k1, p1, k2, p2, k2, p1, k1, p2, p2tog, k1, turn work

Row 7: S1, mb, k2, p1, mb, p2, k2, p2, mb, p1, k2, mb, ssk, k1, turn work

Row 8: S1, p4, k1, p1, k2, p2, k2, p1, k1, p3, p2tog, p1, turn work

Row 9: S1, k4, p1, k1, p2, k2, p2, k1, p1, k5

## GUSSET

Round 1 : Pick up 9 sts (previously sl sts along heel flap, k across front sts (k all 28 sts onto the same needle) (K1, p2, 2x), *k2 *k2, p2, k1, p2, rep from*, end k1 pick up 9 sts along the other side of the heel flap on a new needle

Round 2: Needle one (heel): *K1, p1; rep from * 3 times, k1, p2, k2, p2, *k1, p1; rep from * 2 times, to end k1

Needle two: P1, *mb, p2, mb, p1

Needle four: K1, ssk, k1, p5

Needle three (front): unless otherwise noted: (K1, p2, 2x), *k2, p2, k1, p2, rep from*, to end k1

Round 3: Needle one: K1, p1, mb, p1, k1, p1, mb, p2, k2, p2, mb, p1, k1, p1, mb, p1, k1

Needle two: P5, k2tog, k1

Needle four: k1, ssk, mb, p2, mb, p1

Round 4: Needle one: *K1, p1; rep from * 3x, k1, p2, k2, p2, *k1, p1; rep from * 2x, to end k1

Needle two: p4, k2tog, k1

Needle three: K1, p2, mb, p2 *k2, p2, mb, p2, rep from* end k1

Needle four: K1, ssk, p4

Round 5: Needle one unless otherwise noted: (K1, p1, 3x), k1, p2, k2, p2, (k1, p1, 3x), k1

Needle two: P3, k2tog, k1

Needle four: K1, ssk, P3

Round 6: Needle two: p2, k2tog, k1

Needle three: K1, p2, k1, p2, *k2, p2, mb, p2, rep from*, to end k1

Needle four: k1, ssk, p2

Round 7: Needle one: K1, p1, mb, p1, k1, p1, mb, p2, k2, p2, mb, p1, k1, p1, mb, p1, k1

Needle two: unless otherwise noted: P2, k2

Needle four: unless otherwise noted: K2, p2

Round 8: Needle three: K1, p2, mb, p2, *k2, p2, mb, p2, rep from*, to end k1

Round 9 & 10: Continue pattern

Round 11: Needle one: K1, p1, mb, p1, k1, p1, mb, p2, k2, p2, mb, p1, k1, p1, mb, p1, k1

Round 12: Needle three: K1, p2, mb, p2, *k2, p2, mb, p2, rep from*, to end k1

Round 13 and 14: Continue pattern

Round 15: Needle one: K1, p1, mb, p1, k1, p1, mb, p2, k2, p2, mb, p1, k1, p1, mb, p1, k1

Round 16 Needle 3: K1, p2, mb, p2, *k2, p2, mb, p2, rep from*, to end k1

Round 17 and 18: Continue pattern

Round 19: Needle one: K1, p1, mb, p1, k1, p1, mb, p2, k2, p2, mb, p1, k1, p1, mb, p1, k1

Round 20: Needle 3: K1, p2, mb, p2, *k2, p2, mb, p2, rep from*, to end k1

*Begin Toe*

Divide sts evenly onto 2 dpn, by adding sts from 2 needles with 4 sts each onto heel needle

Next 8 rows *K1, k2tog, k to last 3 sts, ssk, k1*

Use Kitchener stitch to sew toe tip together. Sew in ends and sew cuff to stocking. Use chain stitch to make varied length decorations with a bobble end. Sew Cuff onto stocking

## APPLIQUÈ TETHER AND HANGER

Make I cord, (but instead of using k sts, use p) until approx 28" long

## Pompoms

Make one brown pompom 1-1/2" diameter
Make one white pompom 1" diameter
Sew pompoms on I-cord, layout in desirable design and fasten together

● ● ●

# Design Tip: BALANCE AND COMPOSITION

Use a variety of décor and furniture in a room to gain a dynamic space. Stay away from keeping everything on the same level as it becomes very monotonous. Vary the furniture combinations and heights to move the eye and keep it interesting. Consider height and depth variation as well. We appreciate items in uneven groups and with negative space (space that is empty) between and around them. That way our eye picks up the grouping with ease. The best way to begin this process is to determine what you are going to use the space for, and design purposefully for those functions. Say the mantra with me, "Form follows function".

Let's talk about balance in a space. Furniture should be placed so that large pieces oppose other large items or so that there is something in the room to visually weigh down the other side, such as a piece of furniture, colorful painting, painted wall, large textural hanging and such. Leave enough space so that the room doesn't feel closed in. If the furniture is too heavy visually, using a light colored, painted piece may be just the thing to give the height needed, anchoring the opposing side of the room, while keeping the open feeling. Negative space or areas of rest, should be planned and not established by accident. It is as important as positive space (furniture placement, rugs, chandeliers, and so forth) or even more so because it is what gives us the space to easily find the areas of interest.

Christmas trees are a large focal point in the room and need to be balanced the same as a large piece of furniture. Furnishings of similar visual weight should be placed in opposition, to balance your new layout. Make sure that the furniture does not steal the show from the tree. If so, you may want to remove it for the holidays. When in doubt, less is always more; every surface does not need to have something on it. Clutter is a bad word, minimalist is a good word. Use composition of furniture, color and texture to create a well balanced design.

# Design Tip: BALANCE AND COMPOSITION CONTINUED

When decorating the dining table, the chandelier over the table should not compete for attention with the table. Think of the table centerpiece and the chandelier composition all together. Your eye will take it in as one, so make sure it is designed as such. Be deliberate when designing the table vignette.

When displaying decorations in a room, it is desirable to position them in different locations within the room. The same goes for decorations, as for furniture, spacing them evenly throughout the space makes the room bland and boring. Intentionally move the eye and compose a subconscious symphony, designing focal points, small areas of interest and color that speak together to create the personality of the room.

BREAKING THE RULE: Now having said that things should not be evenly distributed throughout the room, you may break that rule, but only on purpose and only with the same items in repetition or items laid out in a symmetrical fashion. Less is more, but large furniture or built-ins in a small space, fit in correct proportion, can make a room look larger! Large tiles make a room look larger! Lots of little things tend to look like clutter and a few larger items tend to look well placed. It is all about how the eye perceives the space and how you physically move about in the space. A large mirror or picture can take an average wall and turn it into a superstar.

# Design Tip: TEXTURE AND BALANCE

Just as color can balance a room, so can texture. If you are creating a modern sleek look, then your items will be sleek and shiny with clean lines, but to make it interesting you must add contrast with texture. Velvet and silk marry well together as do cottons and linens. It is always a good rule to stick to formal textures and patterns when creating a formal feel to a space and informal textures and patterns when creating an informal space. Place texture throughout the space. Group texture here and there and use contrasting textures to insure tactile interest. Varying types of textures that go well together, add to the comfort of room, as well as, the design appeal of a space.

The Christmas tree is very textural piece in your home. It is a good idea to have heavy draperies or a large sofa on the other side of the room to help balance the tree in the space. A tree shows a natural element, even if you have a faux tree. Placing other natural elements in the room creates a feeling of bringing the outdoors in. Repetition of elements is a necessary ingredient to provide continuity throughout a space. Are all your decorations in one room or do you have holiday reminders throughout your home? Distributing decoration throughout the house makes for a cohesive design that incorporates a reminder of the season in every room.

**BREKAING THE RULE:** Similar style of textures and patterns you say? Ok, here's the rule breaker; an element of surprise may be added very carefully by intentionally upholstering a traditional chair in a contemporary print, as long as the colors coordinate with the room's color palette. Take a traditional wooden piece of furniture and paint it in a bold and surprising way, as long as it is a color repeated in the room. The reverse is also true of course. A stunning contemporary chaise can sit center stage when upholstered in a traditional herringbone pattern. Once again, breaking the rule on purpose is the key and always in moderation or it will backfire.

# ··· Home Décor

Holidays are notorious for being filled with decorations, however one of the most sophisticated avenues to venture down for Christmas decoration, is by changing out the items normally displayed and used for everyday, such as pillows, every day décor, throws and towels. Bathrooms are normally forgotten about during the holidays or addressed with a decorative nightlight. Is it possible to change out your towels for the holidays and add a new glamour to a room that is used so often? The kitchen is a room that is also frequently overlooked. Special towels, along with items of similar color displayed throughout the room add a festive touch to the hub of your household. For example if you choose to use scarlet towels, prominently display a decorative container of pomegranates on the counter and a vase of red flowers to balance the space.

Changing out the blankets in the bedrooms, along with a poinsettia and a jolly old Santa, immediately changes the environment. Don't over design and use too many decorations. It doesn't take a lot, but addressing each room in your house, with a few touches, brings continuity to your design and holiday cheer throughout. For a more ambitious idea, you may even consider changing out the draperies in your great room for your holiday theme and use the opportunity to have the everyday draperies cleaned.

Lighting should be considered as part of your home décor and addressed as such. Twinkle lights to dramatic colored lights create real substance and sculptural dimension in a space. Use portable lighting or design it to be hard wired into your space if you are starting from scratch. Any time that lighting is considered in holiday decorating, the result always adds another layer of interest, bringing the design to a higher level of refinement.

*Modern dot pillow
shown on page 56.*

# Dot Pillow

● ● ●

*Nothing is more timeless or more current than a circle. The circle refuses to be pigeon-holed into any one style and is at home in every time period across the board, from traditional to contemporary.*
*Inherently elegant, yet simple, it forever wears as a contemporary icon. The circle is duel in nature, living as the most basic of shapes and simultaneously as the most complex of shapes. These dots, culled from all the other polka dots, need not be told they are special. Everyone and their brother already know it!*

● ● ●

Put them on a white leather sofa and viola', tres chic, baby! Tone them down, if you must, by using black or white or any other accent color. Consider letting them have their fun by giving them an air of sophistication, creating them with a variegated novelty fur. Since they are precarious and naturally draw attention to themselves, you may use them to do just that, or if your intention is to have them blend into your room to add texture, you must make them the same color as what they will rest on. Whichever you choose, you will be on the right track, because the end result is intentional and well thought out. Bravo!

# Modern Dot Pillow

NOTE: Both pieces of the round pillow are worked in circular, stockinette stitch (knit all rounds). Increases are made by knitting into the front and back of the stitch.

## MATERIALS

- Yarns: 2 Skeins Lion Brand Fun Fur
- 1 Skein medium weight worsted acrylic
- 5 Double Pointed Needles US # 9 / 5.5mm

- Circular Needles US # 9 / 5.5mm
- June Tailor No Sew Home Décor, Round Pillow
  JoAnn Fabric and Craft Stores
  Gauge: 5 sts = 2"; 7 rows = 2"

## SIDE 1

Using yarn A and yarn B held together as 1 and using double-point needles, cast on 8 stitches. Divide stitches evenly onto 4 needles, and join into a circle, being careful not to twist stitches. Place marker to note beginning of round. Change to circular needles when increased stitch numbers no longer fit comfortably on double-point needles.

Round 1: K to end (8 sts)

Round 2: Inc 1 in every st to end (16 sts)

Rounds 3 & 4: K to end

Round 5: *Knit 1, inc 1; rep from * to end (24 sts)

Rounds 6 and 7: K to end

Round 8: Repeat round 5 (36 sts)

Rounds 9 – 11: K to end

Round 12: *K3, inc1; rep from * to end (45 sts)

Rounds 13 – 15: K to end

Round 16: *Knit 4, Inc 1; rep from * to end (54 sts)

Rounds 17 – 19: K to end

Round 20: *K5, inc1; rep from * to end (63 sts)

Rounds 21 – 22: K to end

Round 23: *Knit 6, Inc 1; rep from * to end (72 sts)

*K9, inc1; rep from * to end (99 sts)

Rounds 24 – 28: K to end

Round 29: *K7, inc1; rep from * to end (81 sts)

Rounds 30: K to end

Round 31: *K8, inc1; rep from * to end (90 sts)

Round 32: K to end

Round 33: *K9, inc1; rep from * to end (99 sts)

Bind off 20 sts, cast on 20 sts (Single yarn cast on is easiest here)

Round 34: *K9, k2tog; rep from * to end (90sts)

Round 35: K to end

Round 36: *K8, k2tog; rep from * to end (81 sts)

Round 37 – 39: K to end

Rounds 40: *K7, inc1; rep from * to end (72 sts)

Round 41: K to end

Rounds 42: *K6, k2tog; rep from * to end (63sts)

Rounds 43 – 45: K to end

Round 46:*K5, k2tog; rep from * (54 sts)

Rounds 47 – 48: K to end

● ● ●

<u>Round 49:</u> *K4, k2tog; rep from * (45 sts)

<u>Rounds 50 – 52:</u> K to end

<u>Round 53:</u> *K3, k2tog; rep from * (36sts)

<u>Rounds 54 – 55:</u> K to end

<u>Round 58:</u> *K1, k2tog; rep from * to end (24 sts)

<u>Rounds 59 – 60:</u> K to end

<u>Round 60:</u> *K1, k2tog; rep from * to end (16 sts)

<u>Round 61:</u> K to end

<u>Round 62:</u> *K2tog to end (8 sts)

<u>Round 63:</u> K to end

Insert pillow. Cut yarn leaving a 6-inch tail. Thread needle with yarn tail, pull through remaining stitches and sew ends in. Stitch the opening shut or sew on zipper, if your skills and desire allow.

# Towel Buddy

• • •

*You are trying to get the kids to do their homework, your spouse will be home soon, Susie still has a 10 page report to complete and Jimmy does not understand his math homework, for that matter neither do you. Aromas of onion and garlic waft through the house while you throw together yet another dinner. In slow motion, little Jane slides by the oven door and brushes alongside the hand towel, (now the slow motion begins), there it goes, dropping, dropping to the floor. You contort your body around the dog, while holding a spoon full of spaghetti sauce, in order to catch the towel from hitting the floor. Ker plunk! Another one bites the dust.*

*I included a pattern for a towel buddy to alleviate this stressful situation from occurring, during our most exhausting time of the day, when we are at our most vulnerable. This would make a thoughtful hostess gift. I also like the towel buddy for Grandma, the piano teacher, school teacher, or make a couple to have an extra gift on hand. How wonderful to be able to give a useful, handmade gift.*

• • •

This is a reversible towel holder. Reversible meaning that if you take it as shown and look at the back you will find a graphic everyday pattern, which makes these holders useful, year round. The wrong side of the piece will show long carryovers of yarn. If this is troublesome for you, solid knitted squares could be sewn over them. It does not show and you do not see the wrong side when in use, so it's a personal preference call.

# Towel Buddy

NOTE: White Yarn = wht; Green Yarn = gr

## MATERIALS

- Needles: # 7 / 4.5mm
- Yarn: Worsted weight #4 in any color or brand of
  your choice

  Gauge: 1" = 6 rows; 1" = 4 sts

  Work in moss stitch unless otherwise noted.

## MAKING THE TOWEL BUDDY
**With A cast on 35 sts**
**Begin with right side**

Row 1 – 8: *K1, p1; rep from * to end

Row 9: (K1,p1, 2x) k1, attach wht yarn k11, pu gr k1, p1, k1, pu wht k11, pu gr *k1, p1, 2x) k1

Row 10: (K1, p1, 2x), k1, p5, pu wht p1, pu gr p5, k1, p1, k1, p5, pu wht p1, pu gr p5, k1, (p1, k1, 2x)

Row 11: (K1, p1, 3x), k4, pu wht k1, pu gr k4, (p1, k1, 2x) p1, k4, pu wht k1, pu gr k4, (p1, k1, 3x)

Row 12: (K1, p1, 3x), pu wht p9, pu gr k5, pu wht p9, pu gr (p1, k1, 3x)

Row 13: (K1, p1, 3x), k4, pu wht k1, pu gr k4, (p1, k1, 2x), p1, k4, pu wht k1, pu gr k4, p1, (k1, p1, 2x) k1

Row 14: (K1, p1, 3x), k1, p3, pu wht p1, p3, (k1, p1, 3x), k1, pp3, pu wht p1, pu gr p3, (k1, p1, 3x), k1

Row 15: (K1, p1, 3x), k1, pu wht k7, pu gr (k1, p1, 3x), k1, pu wht k7, (k1, p1, 3x), k1,

Row 16: (K1, p1, 3x), k1, p3, pu wht p1, pu gr p3, (k1, p1, 3x), k1, p3, pu wht p1, pu gr p3, (k1, p1, 3x), k1

Row 17: (K1, p1, 4x), k2, pu wht k1, pu gr k2, (p1, k1, 4x), p1, k2, pu wht k1, pu gr k2, (p1, k1 4x)

Row 18: (K1, p1, 3x), k1, p3, pu wht p1, pu gr p3, (k1, p1, 3x), k1, p3, pu wht p1, pu gr p3, (k1, p1, 3x), k1

Row 19: (K1, p1, 4x), pu wht k5, pu gr p1, (k1, p1, 4x), pu wht k5, pu gr (p1, k1, 4x)

Row 20: (K1, p1, 5x), pu wht p1, pu gr (p1, k1, 6x) p1, pu wht p1, pu gr (p1, k1, 5x)

Row 21: (K1, p1, 4x), k2, pu wht k1, pu gr k2, (p1, k1, 4x), p1, k2, pu wht k1, pu gr k2, (p1, k1, 4x)

Row 22: (K1, p1, 5x), pu wht p1, pu gr (p1, k1, 6x), p1, pu wht p1, pu gr (p1, k1, 5x)

Row 23: (K1, p1, 4x) k1, pu wht k3, pu gr k1, (p1, k1, 5x), k1, pu wht k3, pu gr (k1, p1, 4x), k1

Row 24: (K1, p1, 5x), pu wht p1, pu gr (p1, k1, 6x), p1, pu wht p1, pu gr  (p1, k1, 5x)

Row 25: (K1, p1, 4x), k2, pu wht k1, pu gr (k2, p1, 5x), k2, pu wht k1, pu gr k2, (p1, k1, 4x)

Row 26: (K1, p1, 5x), pu wht p1, pu gr (p1, k1, 6x), p1, pu wht p1, pu gr (p1, k1, 5x)

Rows 27, 29, 31, 33, 35: *K1, p1; rep from * to end

Rows 28, 30, 32, 34, 36: *P1, k1; rep from * to end

Row 37 and all odd Rows to 53: (P1, k1, 3x), p1, pu wht k3, pu gr (p1, k1, 3x), pu wht k3, pu gr (k1, p1, 3x), pu wht, k3, pu gr (p1, k1, 4x)

Row 38 and all even Rows to 54: (P1, k1, 3x), p1, pu wht p3, pu gr (p1, k1, 3x), pu wht p3, pu gr (k1, p1, 3x), pu wht p3, pu gr (p1, k1, 3x), p1

Row 55 and all odd Rows to 61: *P1, k1; rep from * to end

Row 56 and all even Rows to 60: *K1, p1; rep from * to end

B.O.

To attach the towel holder to towel use clutch pins. Using any adhesive that will attach metal to metal or metal to plastic and fix button or other finding to clutch pin and let dry.  Pin towel in between towel holder with clutches.

•  •  •

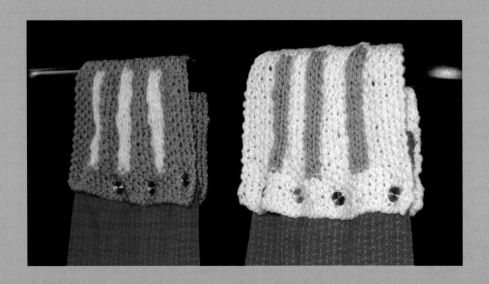

# Rose Candle Décor

• • •

*"A knitted centerpiece?" she muttered in astonishment, "How unusual!" Why not, I dare say. Surrounded by homemade rolls, delectable ham with buttery mashed potatoes and winter squashes, all displayed in the earthiest of handmade pottery, our rose wreath lends, softness in the cornucopia of the holiday. A little glow from a candle in the center creates ambience, enhancing the festiveness of your winter party. People will inevitably ask "Where did you get that?" followed by, "How did you do that?" Exactly what a well-placed conversation piece solicits. Pat yourself on the back and enjoy your party.*

• • •

Gorgeous and unexpected, this candle décor is a very enjoyable, quick project. Mostly knit in stockinette stitch, ( with some basic yarn over's and slip, slip knit for the leaves), calls out this project as a great one for taking the beginning knitter to the next level.

# Rose Candle Decor

NOTE: White Yarn = wht; Green Yarn = gr

## MATERIALS

- 1 Skein Worsted Weight Red
- 3 Skeins coordinating greens
- 1 – 12" Styrofoam Wreath
- Needles Size US #4 / 3.5mm

## MAKING THE ROSE CANDLE DECOR

### WREATH COVER

Cast on 34 stitches work in St. Stitch until desired length.

Cover Styrofoam Wreath and stitch seams

### LEAVES

Cast on 5 sts

Row 1: K to end
Row 2: P to end
Row 3: *Inc1, k1, yo, k1, yo, k1, inc1 (9 sts)
Row 4, 6, 8, 12, 14, 18 & 20: P to end
Row 5 & 11: K4, yo, k1, yo, k5 (11 sts)
Row 7 & 13: K5, yo, k1, yo, k5 (13sts)
Row 9: B.O. 3 sts, k2, yo, k1, yo, k6 (12 sts)
Row 10: B.O. 3 sts, p8 (9 sts)
Row 15: B.O. 3 sts, k9 (10 sts)
Row 16: B.O. 3 sts, p6 (7 sts)
Row 17: Skp, k3, k2tog (5 sts)

Row 19: Skp, k1, k2tog (3 sts)
Row 21: Sk2p, fasten off

### ROSES

Cast on 4 sts

Knit in stockinette st until piece measures 18".
Make 3 pieces

Coil the red roses and tack as necessary. Twist them here and there and form them into roses. Place all three roses evenly distributed. Then sew on the leaves.

• • •

# $\cdots$ Wreaths

A never ending circle of beauty; whether it adorns your holiday door or decorates your table as the centerpiece, there is nothing that pulls at our primal heartstrings like a wreath.  Wrapping twigs, leaves, flowers and other parts of nature into a circle feels natural.  In ancient Persian cultures, wreaths were believed to be a symbol of importance and success.  In Greece, athletes were adorned with wreaths made of laurel for winning events during the Olympic Games.  The eternal circle of a wreath reminds us that souls are immortal and life everlasting.
It seems a natural transition to want to knit a wreath.  The warmth of a cozy wreath on a door is a super comforting image to make family and friends feel welcomed, inside a home.
With that said, do not sit on your Laurels!  Create a circle of cozy warmth for your home.

*Cable Wreath shown on page 78.*

# Pom Pom Wreath

• • •

*Obviously this pompom girl is the queen bee of wreaths!  She is a full figured, boda-
cious beauty that people can't keep their hands off.  Given her cheerful personality, she
is an impeccable choice for welcoming guests into your home.*

• • •

This project is a lot of the same thing over and over.  This offers a good opportunity to get the kids
involved.  Using the pompom makers, everyone can contribute, without it looking like there were many
creators.  In fact this is the most perfect first time knitting project, because although the knitted base is
important as the foundation, it will never be seen!
Love this project for the simplicity of creation, the impactful final product and the meditative advantage.
This one takes the cake as far as a first time project and beats a misshapen potholder hands down.  It's so
much fun; you'll want to make more than one!

# Pom Pom Wreath

NOTE: Increases are made by knitting into the front and back of the stitch.

## MATERIALS

- 1 –16" Styrofoam Wreath
- 3 Skeins Main Color
- 1 Skein Accent Color

- Sizes 85, 65, 45, 35, 115 Pompom makers
- Needles Size US #8 / 5.0mm

**Cast on 28 sts**

Work in stockinette st until piece is long enough to cover wreath

Sew onto the wreath with the seam in back. Sew on Pom Poms.

Make as many pompoms as you see fit. Follow manufacturers directions.

Position the Green Pompoms or whatever color you are using for the accent color, and then fill in with Red Pompom's or whatever color you are using for the main color.

Place pompoms close together for a full, luscious wreath.

Make a variety of pompoms, Sizes 85, 65, 45, and 35 in Red

Make 3 pompoms in green or whatever color you are using for the accent color.

Sizes 115

## GOOD TO KNOW

Consider that this wreath leaves a big impression, so choose colors accordingly. Think of the color of the wall or door that it will adorn. Side by side doors should carry two wreaths of the same color. Choose one main color and one or two at the most accent colors for a bold statement or consider a variety of greens or reds for the main body to give it more dimensions. This is a perfect project to use up left over yarn. Just make sure that the greens, reds, or whatever color you are using are in the same family of colors.

Wool will make for a puffier pom pom, but acrylic works well also. Different yarns have different textures and when mixed together can be interesting or the combination might fight each other for attention. Play around with it and create an original for your family or friends. This would be a great donation for the church or school gala or raffle!

# Squiggle Wreath

• • •

*This gorgeous wreath has a design twist that grabs attention. People want to touch it, because of its warm, bulky, tactile quality, as well as try to figure out how it's made, because of the interesting way that it is engineered. This wreath would be a festive addition to any Christmas décor or an absolutely cherished gift.*

• • •

First place prize goes to this impressive beginner project that is fast and easy, all done in the stockinette stitch.

# Squiggle Wreath

NOTE: used a worsted weight 4 ply 100% acrylic for the dark green wreath cover, inside and outside rings. I used a 3 ply, 100% wool for the center layer and the bow.

## MATERIALS

- 1 – 12" Styrofoam Wreath, may be made with any sized wreath
- A few ounces of red (great use for leftover yarn)
- Needles Size US #8 / 5.0mm

- Yarns: 1 Skein light green,
- 1 Skein, 1 pound Caron, dark green, 100% Acrylic, 16 oz / 453.6g
- Gauge: 6 sts = 2"; 7 rows - 2"

## WREATH COVER
**Cast on 34 stitches work in St.**

Stitch until desired length.
Cover Styrofoam Wreath and stitch seams

## WREATH
Cast on 10 stitches
St. Stitch for 11'- 6"

When piece measures about 3 feet, attach yarn and sew in running stitch, down the center of the knitted strip, (approx 1" stitches), gather strip up and continue to knit and continue to sew the running stitch, until piece is the desired dimension for around the outside of the wreath. Then complete the next wreath rows in the same fashion, measuring as you go.

Sew on gathered strips. Tack where necessary to make secure.

## BOW
**Cast on 5 sts**

Stockinette st for 3 rows, start with p stitch

Row 1 - 3 Stockinette st, start with right side

Row 4: Inc 1, p until last st, inc 1

Row 5: K to end

Rows 6 – 18: repeat Row 7 & 8

Rows 38 – 52: Stockinette st

Rows 53 - 56: P2tog, p until last 2 sts, k2tog

Rows 56 - 59: stockinette st

Rep above 2x

B.O.

## BOW TAIL 1
**Cast on 5 sts**

Row 1 – 8: St. Stitch, (p 1st row)

Row 9: Inc 1, p until last st, inc1 (7 sts)

Row 10: K to end

Row 11: P to end

Row 12: K to end

Row 13 – 20: rep rows 9 – 12 (11 sts)

Row 21: Inc 1, p until last st, inc 1

Row 22: K to end

Row 23: P to end

Row 24: K2tog, k until end of row

Row 25: P until last 2 sts, p2tog

Row 26 – 34: repeat rows 24 & 25

B.O.

**BOW TAIL 2**

**Cast on 5 sts**
Gauge:  6 sts = 2" 7 rows = 2"

Row 1 – 8: Stockinette st, (p 1st row)

Row 9: inc 1, p until last st, inc1 (7sts)

Row 10: K to end

Row 11: P to end

Row 12: K to end

Row 13 – 20: repeat Rows 9 – 12 (11sts)

Row 21: Inc 1, p until last st, inc1

Row 22: K to end

Row 23: P to end Row 24: K until last 2 sts, k2tog

Row 25: P2tog, p until end of row

Row 26 – 34: Repeat rows 24 & 25

B.O.

**BOW BUTTON:**

**Cast on 10 st**

Row 1 – 19: Stockinette st

B.O.

Sew Bow together; sew onto wreath tacking in place to secure.

# Cable Wreath

• • •

*"Great Grandma made that wreath. She used to knit into the wee hours of the morning", shared Elisa with her wide-eyed younger sister. The Cabled wreath is a piece that will be treasured and talked about as it is passed down through your family's generations. Such possessions trigger us to remember and share the stories of where we come from, anecdotes about family and memories of the members that are no longer with us.*

• • •

This is a wrap me up, keep me warm and cozy next to the fire kind of wreath. Cables are traditional, old-fashioned and deliciously comforting as they are beautifully heralded on this circular reminder of the season. Truly an unexpected knitted creation, featuring cables meandering around this wreath, remind us of the circles of love that we cherish in our lives.

# Cable Wreath

NOTE: Increases are made by knitting into the front and back of the stitch.

## MATERIALS

- 1 – 12" Styrofoam Wreath, may be made with any Yarns: 1 Skein Worsted Weight Dark Green,

- Wool Yarn for Felting, Color: Red

- Needles: US # 8 / 5.0mm
  Gauge: 6 sts = 2" 7 rows = 2"

**Cast on 44 Dark Green, 15 Light Green**
Wrong Side

Row 1: Lt. Gr. P5, k2, p6, k2, Dk. Gr. k2, (p4, k9, 2x), k2, p5

Row 2: Dk. Gr. K5, p2, sl next 3 to dpn in front, k3, k3dpn, k3, p4, sl next 3 to dpn in front, k3, k3dpn, k3, p4, sl next 3 to dpn in front, k3, k3dpn, k3, p2 Lt. Gr. p2, sl2dpn, in front, k2, k2 from dpn, k2, p2, k5

Row 3: Lt. Gr. P5, k2, p6, k2 Dk. Gr. k2, (p9, k4, 2x), p9, k2, p5

Row 4: Dk. Gr. K5, p2,(k9, p4, 2x), k9, p2 Lt. Gr. p2, k2, sl2 to dpn hold in back k2, k2 from dpn, p2, k5

Row 5: Lt. Gr. P5, k2, p6, k2 Dk. Gr. k2, (p9, k4, 2x), p9, k2, p5

Row 6: Dk. Gr. K5, p2, k3, slp3dpn, hold in back, k3, k3dpn, p4, k3, slp3 to dpn, hold in back, k3, k3 from dpn, p4, k3, slp3 to dpn, hold in back, k3, p2 Lt. Gr. p2, slp2 to dpn hold in front k2, k2 from dpn, k2, p2 k5

Row 7: Lt. Gr. P5, k2, p6, k2, Dk. Gr. k2, (p9, k4, 2x), p9, k2, p5

Row 8: Dk. Gr. K5, p2, k9, (p4, k9, 2x), p2 Lt. Gr. p2, k2, sl2 to dpn hold in back, k2, k2 from dpn, p2, k5

Repeat Rows 1-8 till desired length

By making this bow in 4 sections, they must be sewn together and it seems to reinforce the structure of the bow. 4 are required

Cast on 5 sts

Stockinette st for 6 rows, start with p stitch (wrong side)

Row 7: Inc 1, p until last st, inc 1

Row 8: K to end

Rows 9 – 21: repeat Row 7 & 8

Rows 22 – 40: Stockinette st

B.O.

## HOLLY

**Cast on 5 st**

**Work 2 rows stockinette st**

Row 1: (RS) Inc 1, k1, yo, k1, yo, k1, inc 1 (9 sts)

Rows 2, 4, 6, 10, 12, 16, 18: Purl to end

Row 3 & 9: K4, yo, k1, yo, k4, (11 sts)

Row 5 & 11: k5, yo, k1, yo, k5 (13 sts)

Row 7: BO 3 sts, k2, yo, k1, yo, k6 (12 sts)

Row 8: Bind off 3 st, p8 (9 sts)

Row 13: Bind off 3 st, k9 (10 sts)

Row 14: Bind off 3 st, p6 (7 sts)

Row 15: Skp, k3, k2tog (5 sts)

Row 17: Skp, k1, k2tog (3 sts)

Row 19: Sk2p, fasten off, sew in ends

## BERRIES

**MB - Cast on 1 st k in front, back, front, back and front again of st (5 sts made in 1st)**

**Turn**

Row 1 & 3: K to end

Row 2: P to end

Row 4: P2tog, p1, p2tog (3st)

Row 5: K

Row 6: P3tog fasten off

## MORE BERRIES

**Cast on 1**

Row 1: K into 3x, (back, front and back again, 3sts)

Row 2: *P; repeat from * to end

Row 3: *K; repeat from * to end

Row 4: *P; repeat from * to end

Row 5: K3, yo (2x)

## BOW

**Cast on 6 st**

Row 1 & 2: Stockinette st

Row 3: Inc 1, k1, yo, k2, ko, k1, inc 1

Row 4, 6, 8: P to end

Row 5: K4, yo, k2, yo, k4

Row 7: K5, yo, k2, yo, k5

Row 9: Sl 1, k5, yo, k2, yo, k6

Row 10, 12, 14, 16, 18, 20, 22: Sl 1, p to end

Row 11: Sl 1, k6, yo, k2, yo, k7

Row 15: Sl 1, k8, yo, k2, yo, k9

Row 17: Sl 1, k9, yo, k2, yo, k10

Row 19: Sl 1, k10, yo, k2, yo, k11

Row 21: Sl 1, k11, yo, k2, yo, k12

Row 23: Sl 1, k12, yo, k2, yo, k13

Row 24: Sl 1, p to end

Row 25: Sl 1, k to end

Row 26: Sl 1, p to end

B.O.

## BOW BUTTON

**Cast on 3**

Row 1 & 2: Stockinette st

Row 3: Inc 1, yo, k1, yo, inc 1

Rows 4, 6, 8, 10, 12: P to end

*Note Rows*

Rows 5 – 11 (odd rows): K2tog, k1, yo, k1, yo, k1 k2 tog

Row 12: K2tog, k3, k2tog

Row 13: P to end

Row 14: K2tog, k1, k2tog

B.O.

## TAIL 1

**Cast on 3**

Row 1 & 2: Stockinette st

Row 3: Inc 1, yo, k1, yo, inc 1

Row 4 - 20 (even): P to end

Rows 5, 7, 9: K2 tog, k1, yo, k1, yo, k1, k2 tog

Row 11: K3, yo, k1, yo, k3

Row 15: K4, yo, k1, yo, k4

Row 17: K5, yo, k1, yo, k5

Row 19: K6, yo, k1, yo, k6

Rows 21-29 (odd): Ssk, k to end

Rows 22-30 (even): P to last 2 sts, p2tog

Row 31: K2 tog, k1

B. O.


## TAIL 2

**Cast on 3**

Row 1 & 2: Stockinette st

Row 3: Inc 1, yo, k1, yo, inc 1

Row 4 - 20 (even): P to end

Rows 5, 7, 9: K2tog, k1, yo, k1, yo, k1, k2tog

Row 11: K3, yo, k1, yo, k3

Row 15: K4, yo, k1, yo, k4

Row 17: K5, yo, k1, yo, k5

Row 19: K6, yo, k1, yo, k6

Row 21 - 29 (odd): K to last 2 sts end k2tog

Rows 22 - 30 (even): Ssp, P to end

Row 31: K2tog, k1

B. O.


Sew bow together, sew knot around bow, sew on tails, and fasten ends.

## RED LEAVES

**Using large needkes, felting wool CO 60 sts**

K until piece measures 12"
Foll felting process

● ● ●

# Fuzzy Wreath

• • •

*"She has fabulous taste, did you see that stunning wreath?" one woman quipped to her friend. Exquisite, it looks like a prop that a model would be strutting down the runway with!" her friend responded. This wreath screams fashion. Total contemporary show stopper, it must be placed all by itself to soak up the limelight. There are many variegated, as well as solid colored faux fur yarns on the market. Play around with different colors. So go on, express yourself, strike a pose and make it your own.*

• • •

Create this gorgeous wreath with contrasting yarn to create depth within the piece. Variegated fur will add a sense of dimension, as will, contrasting the base yarn with the novelty yarn. Brown on brown, black on black or white on white will show as a rich solid color with heavy texture. There are a plethora of colors and textures of yarns on the market to experiment with, if you please.

# Fuzzy Wreath

NOTE:  I used a fairly bulky worsted weight yarn.  If you are using a lighter weight yarn, use smaller needles so that the Styrofoam doesn't show through.  The width of the piece should be 9".

## MATERIALS

- 1 – 16" Styrofoam Wreath
- 3 Skeins Fun Fur

- 1 Skein worsted weight
  Gauge: 4" = 10 sts; 4" = 12 rows
- Needles Size US #8 / 5.0mm

## WREATH COVER

Cast on 22 stitches with both yarns, work in St Stitch until desired length.

Cover Styrofoam Wreath and stitch seams.  Leave as is or add ornaments, bows , silk flowers or whatever tickles your fancy.

# ··· Evergreen Trees

Evergreen trees and bushes, add visual interest and color to winter's landscapes. Evergreen pines visually add warmth and by offering boughs with which to hold snow, they bring calm and quiet to our winters. These trees will cozy-up any winter village scene. They make a bold statement as a beautiful centerpiece on a table runner or in a group as a restful forest for your eyes to gaze upon. Each tree has its own personality and together the winged boughs, the bobble trees and the ruffle trees have differing textures that contrast one another and are acctractive when displayed together. Varying the heights of the trees and arranging them in odd numbers, make for an interesting composition.

*Winged Bough Trees*
*shown on page 91.*

# Ruffle Tree

NOTE: The following pattern is made for a 15" Cone.
For 12" Cone use 28", 26", 22", 20", 18", 16", 10",
For 9" Cone 28", 26", 22", 16", 10""

## MATERIALS

- 1 Skein, Loops and Threads impeccable worsted weight net wt 4.5 oz. 128g, 268 yds/245m 100% Acrylic Yarn or any worsted weight yarn

- Needles US # 4 / 3.5mm
  Cones sizes 9", 12", 15"
  Gauge 2" = 8 sts; 10 rows = 2"

## MAKING THE RUFFLE TREE
### Cast on 10 sts

K in stockingette st until piece measures as follows for each 8 tiers 28", 26", 24", 22", 20", 18", 16", 10".

String yarn through toward one edge of each piece, approx 1 st in from the edge, toward the center, in a ¾" running stitch style. Knot one end of yarn, pull gently to slide your material in small waves toward the knotted end of your yarn. When the knitted strip has been "gathered" to the length you want, sew in ends. Sew ends together and slide over cone. Tack as necessary. Continue until cone is covered.

• • •

# Winged Bough Tree

NOTE: The following pattern is made for a 16" Cone.
For 14" Cone use Bottom Tier One, Tier Three, Tier Four, Tier Five, Tier Six, Top Tier
For 12" Cone use Bottom Tier One, Tier Three, Tier Six and Top Tier.

## MATERIALS

- Loops and Threads impeccable worsted net wt 4.5 oz. 128g 100% Acrylic Yarn

- Needles: US # 4 / 3.5mm
- Cones sizes 9", 12", 15"
  Gauge 2" = 8 sts; 10 rows = 2"

## MAKING THE WINGED BOUGH TREE

### BOTTOM TIER ONE
Cast on 49 sts

Rows 1, 3 and 5: (WS) K1, *yo, k4, p3tog, k4, yo, k1; rep from * to end.

Rows 2, 4 and 6: K1, *yo, p4, p3tog, p4, yo, k1; rep from * to end.

Rows 7, 9 and 11: P2tog, *k4, yo, k1, yo, k4, p3tog; rep from * to end p2tog

Rows 8, 10 and 12: P2tog, *p4, yo, k1, yo, p4, p3tog rep from * to end p2tog.

Row 13: *K10, k2tog; rep from * end k7

Row 14: K to end

Row 15: *K2tog, k10; rep from * end k7

B.O.

### TIER TWO
Same as above through Row 12

Row 13: *K8, k2tog; rep from * end k1

Row 14: *k4, k2tog; rep from * end k3

Row 15: K to end

B.O.

## TIER THREE
**Same as Bottom tier through row 12**

Row 13: *K3, k2tog; rep from * end k4
Row 14: K to end
Row 15: *K3, k2tog; rep from * to end
B.0.

## TIER FOUR
**Same as Bottom tier through Row 12**

Row 13 *K4, k2tog; rep from * to end k1
Row 14 K to end
Row 15 *K4, k2tog; rep from * to end k1
B.0.

## TIER FIVE
**Same as Bottom tier through Row 12**

Row 13: *K2, k2tog; rep from * to end k1
Row 14: K to end
Row 15: *K2, k2tog; rep from * to end k1
B.0.

## TIER SIX
**Same as Bottom tier through Row 12**

Row 13: *K2, k2tog; rep from * to end k1
Row 14: K to end
Row 15: *K2tog; rep from * to end
B.0.

## TIER SEVEN
**Same as Tier Six**

## TOP TIER EIGHT
**Same as Bottom Tier through Row 12**

B.0.

Sew pieces together and slide over cone. Remember to sew the top shut on the top tier then place on top like a little hat. Tack tiers in place.

# Bobble Tree

NOTE: *For a 12" Use Tier Seven, Six, Four, Two and One

**For a 9" Use Tier Seven, Six, Three and One

## MATERIALS

- 1 Skein - 128 g/4.5 oz
- 268 yds/245m
- Worsted weight

- Styrofoam Cones sizes 9", 12", 15"
- Needles: US # 4 / 3.5
  Gauge 2" = 8 sts; 10 rows = 2"

## TIER ONE
### Cast on 21 ts

Row 1: P1, Mb, p4, *mb, p4; rep from * to end p4

Row 2: K1, *yo, k3, sk2p, k3, yo, k1; rep from * to end

Row 3: P to end

Row 4: P1, *k1, yo, k2, sk2p, k2, yo, k1, p1; rep from * to end

Rows 5 and 7: K1, p9; rep from * to end k1

Row 6: P1, *K2, yo, k1, sk2p, k1, yo, k2, p1; rep from * to end

Row 8: *k2tog; rep from * to end k1

Row 9: P to end

Row 10: *K2tog; rep from * to end k1

Row 11: P to end

After each tier, draw string through stitches, sew in tail. Sew side up and fasten ends in

## TIER TWO
### Cast on 21 ts

Row 1: P1, Mb, p4, *mb, p4; rep from * to end p4

Row 2: K1, *yo, k3, sk2p, k3, yo, k1; rep from * to end

Row 3: P to end

Row 4: P1, *k1, yo, k2, sk2p, k2, yo, k1, p1; rep from * to end

Rows 5 and 7: K1, p9; rep from * to end k1

Row 6: P1, *k2, yo, k1, sk2p, k1, yo, k2, p1; rep from * to end

Row 8: K1, *k3, yo, sk2p, yo, k4; rep from * to end

Row 9: *P4, p2tog; rep from* to end p6

Row 10: *K4, k2tog; rep from * to end k3

Row 11: P to end

Row 12: K to end

B.O.

## TIER THREE
**Cast on 31 sts**

Row 1: P1, MB, *p4, mb; rep from * to end p2

Row 2: K1, *yo, k3, sk2p, k3, yo, k1; rep from * to end

Row 3: P to end

Row 4: P1, *k1, yo, k2, sk2p, k2, yo, k1, p1; rep from * to end

Rows 5 and 7: K1, p9; rep from * to end k1

Row 6: P1, *k2, yo, k1, sk2p, k1, yo, k2, p1; rep from * to end

Row 8: K1, *k3, yo, sk2p, yo, k4; rep from * to the end

Row 9: P to end

Row 10: *K4, k2tog; rep from * to end k1

Row 11: *P4, p2tog; rep from * to end p4

Row 12: *K3, k2tog; rep from * to end k4

Row 13: *P3, p2tog; rep from *

Row 14: B.0.


## TIER FOUR
**Cast on 31 sts**

Row 1: P1, *Mb, p4; rep from * to end p2

Row 2: K1, *yo, k3, sk2p, k3, yo, k1; rep from * to end

Row 3: P to end

Row 4: P1, *k1, yo, k2, sk2p, k2, yo, k1, p1; rep from * to end

Rows 5 and 7: K1, p9; rep from * to end k1

Row 6: P1, *k2, yo, k1, sk2p, k1, yo, k2, p1; rep from * to end

Row 8: K1, *k3, yo, sk2p, yo, k4; rep from * to end

Row 9: P to end

Row 10: *K4, k2tog; rep from * to end k1

Row 11: *P4, p2tog; rep from * to end p2

Row 12: K to end

Row 13: P to end

Row 14: B.0.


## TIER FIVE
Repeat Tier Four


## TIER SIX
**Cast on 41 sts**

Row 1: P1, *Mb, p4; rep from * to end

Row 2: K1, *yo, k3, sk2p, k3, yo, k1; rep from * to end

Row 3: P to end

Row 4: P1, *k1, yo, k2, sk2p, k2, yo, k1, p1; rep from * to end

Row 5 and 7: K1, p9; rep from * to end k1

Row 6: P1, *k2, yo, k1, sk2p, k1, yo, k2, p1; rep from * to end

Row 8: K1, *k3, yo, sk2p, yo, k4; rep from * to end

Row 9: P to end

Row 10: K1, *k3, yo, sk2p, yo, k4; rep from * to end

Row 11: *P4, p2 tog; rep from * to end p5

Row 12: *K4, k2 tog; rep from * to end k5

Row 13: P to end

Row 14: B.0.

## TIER SEVEN

Cast on 51 sts

Row 1: P1, mb, p4, *mb, p4; rep from * to end p6

Row 2: K1, *yo, k3, sk2p, k3, yo, k1; rep from * to end

Row 3: P to end

Row 4: P1, *k1, yo, k2, sk2p, k2, yo, k1, p1; rep from * end k1, yo, k2, sk2p

Rows 5 and 7: k1, p9; rep from * to end k1

Row 6: P1, *k2, yo, k1, sk2p, k1, yo, k2, p1; rep from * to end

Row 8: P1 *k3, yo, sk2p, yo, k3, p1; rep from * to end

Row 9: P to end

Row 10: K1, *k3, yo, sk2p, yo, k4; rep from * to end

Row 11: *P4, p2 tog; rep from * to end p1

Row 12: *K4, k2 tog; rep from * end k1

Row 13: P to end

Row 14: B.O.

• • •

# ··· Apparel

Aren't we deserving of a little attention?  After spending our energies on decorating our homes, it's time to turn to ourselves.  The holiday season is filled with new dresses, shoes and accessories, why not throw in a couple fabulous hats and wraps, if not for warmth, for the sheer thrill of it.  Tis the season to glam it up a bit and don a new shrug over our favorite black party dress.  The kids are playing outside with friends and feeling great in their hip and trendy new hats.  Best of all, you can be proud that you made them.  It doesn't get any better than that.

*Elegant Wrap shown on*
*page 100.*

# Wraps

• • •

*Throw a soft, elegant wrap around your chilled shoulders and your favorite holiday dress and suddenly you feel like Cinderella going to the ball. Warm and absolutely darling, this will make any young lady's demeanor change instantly, as she considers herself, all grown up. Mom will want to join in on the fun and make a matching shrug for herself. Breathtaking all on its own, leave it as is or add a gorgeous pin for a bit of pizzazz.*

• • •

Versatile, warm and lovely describes this faux fur wrap. This virtual chameleon takes on new looks with numerous ways to tie it, throw it, wrap it. An easy on and off type of wrap, perfect for (shall we say) extreme temperature changes. You'll love it! Pair it with jeans and a tee shirt or dress it up for a night on the town with a pretty dress, either way it is befitting.

# Elegant Wrap

NOTE: unless noted knit without novelty yarn, hereafter referred to as ff. When knitting with novelty yarn combine it with the major yarn used in the piece. The major yarn will be referred to as (wh).

## MATERIALS

- Needles: US size #10 /6.0mm

- Loops & Threads, Charisma, Bulky Weight

- Patons Allure, Bulky #5, 100% Nylon, 47 yds/43 meters, 1-3/4 oz/ 50g

  Gauge: 6 sts; 2" 7 rows = 2"

**Cast on 16 sts**

Row 1 (right side): (Ff) k2, (wh) p2, k6, p2, k3, inc 1

Row 2: Inc 1, p4, k2, p6, k2, (ff) p2

Row 3: (Ff) k2, (wh), p2, k6, p2, k5, inc 1

Row 4: Inc 1, (p6, k2, 2x), (ff) p2

Row 5: (Ff) k2, (wh), (p2, k6, 2x), p2, inc 1

Row 6: Inc 1, (k2, p6, 2x), k2, p6, k2, (ff) p2

Row 7: (Ff) k2, (wh), (p2, k6, 2x), p2, k1, inc 1

Row 8: Inc 1, p2, (k2, p6, 2x), k2, (ff) p2

Row 9: (Ff) k2, (wh), (p2, k6, 2x), k3, inc 1

Row 10: Inc 1, p4, (k2, p6, 2x), k2, (ff) p2

Row 11: (Ff) k2, (wh), (p2, k6, 2x), p2, k5, inc 1

Row 12: Inc 1, (p6, k2, 3x), (ff) p2

Row 13: (Ff) k2, (wh), (p2, k6, 3x), p2, Inc 1

Row 14: Inc 1, (k2, p6, 3x), k2, (ff) p2

Row 15: (Ff) k2, (wh), (k6, p2, 3x), k1, inc 1

Row 16: Inc 1, p2, k2, (p6, k2, 3x), (ff) p2

Row 17: (Ff) k2, (wh), (p2, k6, 3x), p2, k3, inc 1

Row 18: Inc 1, p4, (k2, p6, 3x), k2, (ff) p2

Row 19: (Ff) k2, (wh), (p2, k6, 3x), p2, k5, inc 1

Row 20: Inc 1, (p6, k2, 4x), (ff) p2

Row 21: (Ff) k2, (wh), (p2, k6, 4x), p2, inc 1

Row 22: Inc 1, (k2, p6, 4x) k2, (ff) p2

Row 23: (Ff) k2, (wh), (p2, k6, 4x), p2, (ff) k2

Row 24: (Ff), p2, (k2, p6, 4x), k2, (ff) p2

Row 25: (Ff) k2, (wh), (p2, k6, 4x), p2, (ff) k2

Repeat rows 24 & 25 until piece measures 32" or desired width around shoulders. Begin on a wrong side row.

## Begin Decreasing

Row 1 (wrong side): K2tog, (k2, p6,4x), k2, (ff) p2

Row 2: (Ff) k2, (wh), (p2, k6, 4x), p2, k2tog

Row 3: K2tog, (p6, k2, 4x), k2, (ff) p2

Row 4: (Ff) k2, (wh), (p2, k6, 3x), p2, k5, k2tog

Row 5: K2tog, p4, (k2, p6, 3x), k2, (ff) p2

Row 6: (Ff) k2, (wh), (p2, k6, 3x), p2, k3, k2tog

Row 7: K2tog, (k2, p6, 3x), k2, (ff) p2

Row 8: (Ff) k2, (wh), (p2, k6, 3x), p2, k1, k2tog

Row 9: K2tog, (k2, p6, 3x), k2, (ff) p2

Row 10: (Ff) k2, (wh), (p2, k6, 3x), p2, k2tog

Row 11: K2tog, (p6, k2, 3x), k2, (ff) p2

Row 12: (Ff) k2, (wh), (p2, k6, 2x), p2, k5, k2tog

Row 13: K2tog, p4, (k2, p6, 2x), k2, (ff) p2

Row 14: (Ff) k2, (wh), (p2, k6, 2x), k3, k2tog

Row 15: K2tog, p2, (k2, p6, 2x), k2, (ff) p2

Row 16: (Ff) k2, (wh), (p2, k6, 2x), p2, k1, k2tog

Row 17: K2tog, (k2, p6, 2x), k2, (ff) p2

Row 18: (Ff) k2, (wh), (p2, k6, 2x), p2, k2tog

Row 19: K2tog, (p6, k2, 2x), (ff) p2

Row 20: (Ff) k2, (wh), p2, k6, p2, k5, k2tog

Row 21: K2tog, p4, k2, p6, k2, (ff) p2

Row 22: (Ff) k2, (wh), p2, k6, p2, k3, k2tog

### CENTER PIECE OF WRAP

**Cast on 12 sts**

Row 1: (Ff) k2, (wh), p2, k4, p2, (ff) k2

Row 2: (Ff) p2, (wh), k2, p4, k2, (ff) p2

Repeat rows 1 & 2 till piece measures approx 6″

Sew Wrap together, making sure not to twist.
Sew Centerpiece around seam. Fasten all ends in.

# Furry Wrap

NOTE: *Fancy!  Sophisticated!  All the perks of fur, with out the guilt!  Feel like a movie star in this delightful wrap

## MATERIALS

- **Fun Fur or Novelty Yarn of Your Choice**
- **White Acrylic Yarn Worsted Weight**
- **Needles: US #10 / 6.0mm**

**For Children's Size: Cast on 28 sts**

**For Adult's Size: Cast on 56 sts**

Using both yarns knit in stockinette st until piece wraps around comfortably.
B.O.
Fasten in ends.  Clasp with favorite brooch or tie shut.

# Evening Bag

## MATERIALS

- Yarn: #2 Fine, Sport Baby Weight

- Needles: 5 dpn's US 5 / 3.75mm

**Cast on 52 sts onto 4 dpn's, (move sts onto next needle as necessary), place marker to mark the beginning of the round.**

Row 1: K2, *yo, k1-b, yo, ssk, k5; rep from *, end k2

Row 2: K5, *k2tog-b, k7*; rep from*, end, k2tog-b, k6

Row 3: K2, *yo, k1-b, yo k2, ssk, k3; rep from *, end k2

Row 4: *K7, k2tog-b; rep from *, end k4

Row 5: K2, *k1-b, yo, k4, ssk, k1, yo; rep from *, end k2

Row 6: K1, *k7, k2tog-b; rep from *, end k3

Row 7: K2, *k5, k2tog, yo, k1-b, yo; rep from *, end k2

Row 8: K6, *k2tog, k7; rep from *, end k5

Row 9: K2, *k3, k2tog, k2, yo, k1-b, yo: rep from *, end k2

Row 10: K4, *k2tog, k7; rep from *

Row 11: K2, *yo, k1, k2tog, k4, yo, k1-b; rep from *, end k2

Row 12: K3, *k2tog, k7; rep from *, end k1

Repeat row 1-12 3x

*Begin Bottom*

I wanted to make this pattern accessible to more knitters so I have chosen to finish the bottom in the following way. If you are a more advanced knitter, you may finish the bottom by double knitting the 3" bottom, binding off, then cut a textile board bottom to size and slip into the pocket, stitch up seam.

K 12 sts, BO remainder sts keeping last stitch on the needle.

K the 13 sts in stockinette pattern for 3"

Sew the 3 sides of the flap to make the bottom, insert textile board bottom and tack down.

Cut 3/8" ribbon of your choice and weave through the lace pattern of the purse approx 1" from the top, tie to shut.

Tack a fabric gift bag pouch to inside of bag for a lining (if you can find one that fits well), or cut a 12" diameter circle out of a lining weight material, roll over edges and stitch. Stitch ¼" beneath in a wide running stitch and gather up. Sew over top to secure and tack into purse. Make sure that you leave lots of stretch in the purse.

Attach handle, strap or ribbons to finish off.

# Beanie and Stocking Cap

• • •

*"Make me one of those!" says everyone. Cute, stylish, and hip, they are suitable for boys or girls, men and women. Beanie's are in and these colors are hot. Here's a trendy new take on the old-fashioned stocking cap which makes this cap fun and funky. Make one of these for everyone and they will love you for it!*

• • •

Hats that knit up this fast tend to be great fun. This is an easy to knit pattern that you will want to make for all the grandkids or nieces and nephews. What a terrific way to use up leftover yarn, while having fun putting together many color combinations. White with blues will have such a different look than even browns with blues. Getting carried away with color relationships, creating varying looks from one simple pattern makes this one easy to get addicted to.

p. 107

# Stocking Cap

NOTE: Girls/Boys One Size Fits All

## MATERIALS

- **Double Pointed Needles US # 7 / 4.5mm**
- **1 Skein of each color Worsted Weight Yarn**

Gauge 2" = 7 sts; 2" = 9 rows

### Cast on 58 sts with blue yarn

Knit in k2, p2 rib pattern for 2"
Attach orange yarn knitting in rib pattern for 1"
Attach green yarn knitting in rib pattern for 7-1/2"
Attach orange yarn knitting in rib pattern for ¾"
Attach green yarn knitting in rib pattern for 2"
Attach blue yarn knitting in rib pattern for ½"
Attach green yarn knitting in rib pattern for 4"

*K2, p2tog; rep from* to end
*K1, p1; rep from* to end
*K2tog; rep from* to end
Pull yarn through rem sts
Sew in ends
Make pompom, sew on top

• • •

# Beanie

NOTE: Girls/Boys One Size Fits All

## MATERIALS

- Double Pointed Needles US #7 / 4.5mm
- 1 Skein of each color Worsted Weight Yarn

Gauge 2" = 7 sts ; 2" = 9 rows

**Cast on 44 Dark Green, 15 Light Green**
**Cast on 58 sts with blue yarn**

Knit in k2, p2 rib pattern for 2"

Attach orange yarn knitting in rib pattern for 1"
Attach green yarn knitting in rib pattern for 4"

*K2, p2tog; rep from* to end
*K1, p1; rep from* to end
*K2tog; rep from* to end

Pull yarn through rem sts
Sew in ends

• • •

# Sources for Supplies

Usually the supplies you need for making the projects in this book can be found at your local craft supply stores, discount marts, home improvement centers, hardware stores (snow people parts) or retail shops. Occasionally, you may choose to, or need to buy materials or tools from specialty yarn stores.

Local knitting stores will be able to provide good felting wool. It is in our best interest as knitters to support our local yarn shops, so that we may have access to the wonderful world of beautiful, unique yarns and accessories. The yarn chosen for the patterns in this book are designed to be, and encouraged to be interchangeable with similar yarns. The hope is that through instruction given in the book, you are more willing to experiment with your own color combinations and textures.

In order to provide you with the most up to date information, we have created a list of suppliers on our website, which we update on a regular basis. Visit us at HYPERLINK "http://www.needleworkarts.com" www.needleworkarts.com, click on "Craft Supply Sources, and the click on the relevant topic. You will find companies listed with their web address and/ or mailing address and phone number.

# ··· Templates

# Leaf Template

# Advent Calendar Number Templates

# Stitch Glossary

**Bobble** —Cast on 1 st, k in front, back, front, back and front again of sts (5sts made in one st). Turn. K 1 row, p 1 row, k 1 row. Next row p2tog, p1, p2tog, (3 sts). K 1 row. P3tog, fasten off.

**Chain stitch** —Make a slip knot and place it around the crochet hook, lay the yarn across the crochet hook, so that you can use the hook to pull it through the loop that is currently on the crochet hook. The first one is the trickiest. After pulling the yarn through the slip knot it remains on the crochet hook, forming a second loop. Rep to desired length.

**Felting** —Place piece to be felted in a pillow case. Tie ends of pillow case together. Wash piece in hot water with a pair of jeans and a Tablespoon of detergent. Check periodically every 5- 10 minutes to make sure it isn't felting too fast. Dry in clothes dryer. Check periodically every 5 minutes to make sure it isn't felting too fast. Continue process and repeat until desired results.

**I cord** —Using dpn's or a short circular needle, cast on 3 sts or number of stitches required.
Row 1: k3, do not turn, slide sts to other end of needle.
Rep row 1 to desired length. BO

**Kitchener stitch** —Insert tapestry needle purlwise through first stitch on front needle. Pull yarn through, leaving that stitch on knitting needle.
Insert tapestry needle knitwise through first stitch on back needle. Pull yarn through, leaving stitch on knitting needle.
Insert tapestry needle knitwise through first stitch on front needle, slip stitch off needle and insert tapestry needle purlwise through next stitch on front needle. Pull yarn through, leaving this stitch on needle.
Insert tapestry needle purlwise through first stitch on back needle. Slip stitch off needle and insert tapestry needle knitwise through next stitch on back needle. Pull yarn through, leaving this stich on needle. Repeat steps 3 and 4 until all stitches on both front and back needles have been grafted. Fasten off and weave in end.

**Pompom** —Follow instructions supplied by pompom maker manufacturer.

# Abbreviations

**approx** – approximately

**beg** – begin(s); beginning

**bc** (back cross) –sl 1 st to dpn and hold in back, k1, then p1 from dpn

**bkc** (back knit cross) – same as bc, but knit both sts

**bpc** (back purl cross) – same as bc, but purl both sts

**BO** – bind off

**cn** – cable needle

**co** – cast on

**c4b** – slip 2 sts onto cn and hold in back. K2, then k2 from cn

**c4f** – slip 2 sts onto cn and hold in front. K2, then k2 from cn

**cont** – continue; continuing

**dec** – decrease; decreasing

**dpn** – double pointed needle

**fc** (front cross) –sl 1 st to dpn and hold in front, p1, then k1 from dpn

**fkc** (front knit cross) – same as fc, but knit both sts

**fpc** (front purl cross) – same as fc, but purl both sts

**gauge** – The number of stitches across and rows up and down in a certain length. Achieving the specified gauge is essential when knitting a pattern.

**g** – grams

**inc(s)** – increasing

**k** – knit

**k2tog** – knit 2 stitches together as one

**k3dpn** – knit 3 stitches from dpn

**kp3** – knit one stitch pass 3 stitches over one at a time.

**mb** – make bobble

**mm** – millimeter(s)

**p** – purl

**pm** – place marker

**p2tog** – purl 2 stitches together as one

**psso** – pass slipped stitch over

**p2sso** – pass 2 slipped stiches over

**pu** – pick up (yarn or stitches)

**rem** – remaining spp – slip one, purl one, pass slip stitch overrep – repeat

**rnd**(s) – round(s)

**sl** – slip

**skp** – slip 1 stitch as if to knit, knit 1, pass slip stitch over

**sk2p** – slip 1 stitch as if to knit, knit two together, pass slipped stitch over

**Sl2dpn** – slip 2 stitches onto dpn

**sp2p** – Slip 1 stitch as if to purl, purl two together slipped stitch over

**ssk** – slip 2 stitches knitwise, one at a time, from the left needle to right needle, insert left needle tip through both front loops and knit together from this position (1 stitch decrease)

**st** – stockinette stitch

**tog** – together

**wyb** – with yarn in back

**wyf** – with yarn in front

**x** – times

**yd** – yard(s)

**yf** – yarn forward

**yo** – yarn over

( ) - Repeat everything in parenthesis the denoted amount of times

# A Note To End On

Anticipation of laughter, good conversation, hours of relaxation and reflection, occupies our dreams, concocting expectations for the holidays. Gathering with friends and family, we rekindle familiar relationships while making new acquaintances. Days are filled with the amusement of watching children eagerly await the magic of Christmas day. Adults dream up grandeur plans of entertaining, being entertained and of what the holidays might offer.

Our days are wrapped around each other with phone calls and shopping sprees; coffee dates and parties, the communication and preparation that will bring our vision together and give our holiday meaning. We focus on reminding ourselves and loved ones of how much we value one another.

Baking cookies, making gifts, decorating our yards and homes create an ambiance to enhance the holiday spirit. We set the stage with a magical atmosphere imagined in our dreams and woven through our holiday designs. It is our home, where we create memories of lifetimes, share joy and sorrow, where our emotion and lives are real.

Our senses are tantalized by aromas of baked goodies, cinnamon, pine, while stimulated visually by an environment that speaks holiday. The sounds of the season greet us throughout our homes and all the places we go to. We can't wait to get our hands on the presents, wrapped with lovely papers and bows, the tempting treats, and if all is well, each other under the mistletoe.

The holidays give us a re-birth, energy charging us with goals and hopes and dreams for the coming year. The holidays are our reason and our opportunity to further develop our relationships with family and friends and to give thanks for all we have. To assess where we are and where we are going. Christmas is a time when we set aside time, spending that time with those that give meaning to our life.

Knit for family, friends and great causes. Soar to the limits of your imagination! I would like to wrap up the hopes and dreams of the holiday season in a warm, cozy, soft knitted, yarn hug, from me to you.

● ● ●